WTO Dispute Settlement

Time to Take Stock

P.I.E. Peter Lang

Bruxelles • Bern • Berlin • Frankfurt am Main • New York • Oxford • Wien

Jacques BOURGEOIS,
Marco BRONCKERS & Reinhard QUICK (eds.)

WTO Dispute Settlement

Time to Take Stock

College of Europe Studies
Vol. 19

With the financial support for the colloquium by Bayer, EGA, Evonik, Pernod Ricard and VCI.

Cover picture: Enrique Mendizabal, Flickr.

The book was subject to a double blind refereeing process.

© P.I.E. PETER LANG s.a.
Éditions scientifiques internationales
Bruxelles, 2017
1 avenue Maurice, B-1050 Bruxelles, Belgique
www.peterlang.com ; brussels@peterlang.com

Imprimé en Allemagne

ISSN 1780-9665
ISBN 978-2-8076-0287-8
ePDF 978-2-8076-0376-9
ePub 978-2-8076-0377-6
Mobi 978-2-8076-0378-3
DOI 10.3726/b11187
D/2017/5678/36

CIP available from the British Library and from the Library of Congress, USA.

Bibliographic information published by "Die Deutsche Nationalbibliothek"
"Die Deutsche Nationalbibliothek" lists this publication in the "Deutsche Nationalbibliografie";
detailed bibliographic data is available on the Internet at <http://dnb.d-nb.de>.

Table of Contents

Introduction

Its dispute settlement system is still regularly referred to as the jewel in the WTO's crown. At the same time, this system has been under review for rather more than half of its existence, and that review has spawned hundreds of proposals for amendment from the WTO membership – although none has been accepted so far.[1] Academics and practitioners have added their fair share of criticisms and calls for improvements over the years. It seemed therefore apposite, when reaching the WTO's 20th anniversary, to perform a "health check" of WTO dispute settlement during a scientific conference: is the system fundamentally in good shape, or are fundamental changes in order?

When designing the conference, the emphasis was indeed on essentials. We did not want to get lost in the myriad of technical issues that easily bedevil any discussion of the WTO's Dispute Settlement Understanding (DSU), or the case law of WTO panels and the WTO Appellate Body.

After a welcoming address by Prof. Monar, Rector of the College of Europe, Prof. Ehlermann, former member of the WTO Appellate Body, gave the keynote speech. He noted "the appalling lack of equilibrium" between the "legislative branch" and the "judicial branch" of the WTO. He referred to the increasing workload of the WTO dispute settlement system and proposed remedies. With foresight, given the crisis that arose later in the spring of 2016 when the United States blocked the re-nomination of the Korean member of the Appellate Body Prof. Seung Wha Chang, Prof. Ehlermann deplored "the denaturation of the selection of Appellate Body members" resulting in part from the shortness of the mandates.[2]

Experts were invited to present papers on five basic themes, and these papers with commentary are reproduced in the volume you now have in front of you. *First*, it did appear useful to start at the beginning, and re-examine the function of WTO dispute settlement. Prof. De Bièvre raised the question whether the function of the WTO dispute settlement was just to settle disputes between Members – to which uncertainties about

---

[1] For a recent assessment of the discussions ahead of the Nairobi Ministerial see the report by the chairman of the WTO Dispute Settlement Body, Ambassador Ronald Saborio Soto, of 4 December 2015 (TN/DS/28).

[2] Prof. Ehlermann elaborated his views in his contribution to the Festschrift for his former colleague on the Appellate Body, Prof. Matsushita: International Economic Law and Governance 26-29 (Chaisse & Lin (eds.), Oxford, 2016).

precedents would point, or to create "jurisprudence" in the broader sense – if so, there is a need for "judicial economy".

In his comments Dr. Ehring focused on the operation of the WTO dispute settlement system in the present circumstances. He characterized them as an era of dysfunctional negotiations in the WTO, an era of protectionism and an era of bilateralism. On the US criticism about "gap filling" by the WTO dispute settlement system he pointed out that is not for individual Members to decide that there are gaps.

Another basic question that received attention in a *second* panel was: what is or should be the applicable law in WTO dispute settlement proceedings? This question arises at the establishment of a panel, being a precondition to the exercise of jurisdiction by the panel, the applicability and the application of rules of law to the facts of a matter. On this latter point Prof. Bartels saw in Article 19:2 of the DSU – panel and Appellate Body may not "add to or diminish" rights and obligations under the covered agreements – "a conflicts rule limiting the uses of what could, *a priori*, be accepted as applicable law". Relying on several Appellate Body reports, Prof. Bartels concluded that it is right for WTO panels and the Appellate Body to apply international law, with the proviso that this may not lead to non-application of valid WTO law.

In her comments, Prof. Footer spoke of the WTO's "institutional schizophrenia", referring to the WTO "legislative's" body inability to come up with authentic interpretations. She noted that there was not enough thinking about conflict rules. She saw in the case law a recognition of "*ne ultra petitum*". She was of the view that "matter" in an Article 21:5 DSU proceeding could be new rather than additional to the matter in the original proceeding.

Before moving on to the last two papers, Prof. Quick addressed several questions on the WTO dispute settlement process to a panel composed of business representatives. The main points made were the following. For business, the rule of law is essential for a stable, predictable climate; business therefore supports a more effective dispute settlement system. Moreover, a concern was expressed about a very narrow attitude on "res inter alios acta", i.e. rulings about Member A measures have no impact on Member B applying similar measures. In addition, the policy of the EU Commission in respect of bringing cases to WTO dispute settlement was questioned: the EU Commission should be braver. Moreover, in the absence of any progress at WTO level, the WTO dispute settlement system should be strengthened through bilateral negotiations. Finally, business should push their own governments to comply with WTO dispute settlement rulings. One business representative focused on TRIPs enforcement and its impact on the relationship between competition policy and IPRs and illustrated this with a series of examples.

A *third* paper analyzed the very end of WTO dispute settlement proceedings: are the current remedies to ensure compliance with WTO rules and rulings satisfactory? Prof. Bronckers and Prof. Baetens situated the WTO's system by drawing comparisons with public international law generally, as well as EU law. In their view the WTO system of remedies is seriously flawed. The authors advocate that financial remedies be added to the DSU, with some retroactive effect, to enhance compliance and avoid the drawbacks of retaliation ("shooting in one's own foot", and damaging "innocent bystanders"). Financial remedies would also serve to re-balance the WTO's dispute settlement system, notably with an eye to the legitimate interests of smaller and developing countries.

In his comments, Prof. Hoekman, speaking as an economist, referred to the drawbacks of retaliation as expounded in the economic literature. He quibbled with the view that governments don't want to retaliate and referred to examples and the FIAM judgment; he also took issue with the view that retaliation never works. He confirmed that, also from an economic point of view, financial payments are much better than retaliation. He elaborated on how this could work. He advocated that small Members act together threatening to retaliate collectively in an effort to persuade a large respondent to pay financial compensation. Prof. Tietje noted that it is wrongly assumed that there is a compliance problem; there are only some pathological situations and cited statistics to that effect. He made the point that "suspension of concessions" has nothing to do with compensation and is meant to re-establish the balance of concessions. Instances of application of Article 22 DSU deal with deeply rooted regulatory matters that have nothing to do with exchange of concessions (Hormones, FSC, Bananas). For Prof. Tietje the best remedy is to give private parties the right to sue the respondent Member. Internalizing the externalities caused by non-compliance at intergovernmental level is only a second-best solution

Given the ascendance of bilateral and regional trade agreements, it was only timely to look at the way these newer agreements envisage the settlement of disputes. The *fourth* paper of Mr. Brown draws a parallel between dispute settlement as arranged in the latest EU Free Trade Agreements and WTO dispute settlement. It also deals with the relationships between these two kinds of dispute settlement regimes and refers in particular to the arrangements in the EU/Korea FTA. In his comments Prof. Kuijper first underlined the need for drawing clear border lines between these two kinds of dispute settlement systems. In his view, the EU should learn from WTO cases that went wrong: in Mexico-High Fructose Syrup the respondent blocked a list of panelists. He advocates a return to the old system of arbitration. On retaliation he made two points: the need for a "no double jeopardy" clause and the principle of "*electa una via, altra non datur*", i.e., no right to seek WTO dispute settlement where one is not happy with the result of a proceeding of an FTA dispute settlement.

In recent years the mechanisms used to resolve disputes between foreign investors and states ("ISDS") have also attracted much attention and controversy. A *fifth* panel questioned whether there is anything here that could inspire reform of the WTO, and conversely are there elements in the WTO's system of settling disputes that could improve ISDS? One key feature in the debate on investor-state dispute settlement is the appointment of arbitrators. Should private parties continue to have the freedom to appoint one of the arbitrators, or should arbitrators be selected exclusively from a list or roster established by governments? In that debate, the experience with the (governmental) appointment of ad hoc panelists in WTO dispute settlement proceedings could be enlightening. This was the subject of an exhaustive analysis by Mrs. Johannesson and Prof. Mavroidis. In her paper Prof. Baetens compared the strengths, weakness, opportunities and threats of the ISDS and WTO systems. She concludes that both systems would benefit from a "look across the border". Finally, Mr. Grierson offered comments from a practitioner's perspective on the points made in the papers on the ISDS process.

As the participants of the conference will realize, publication of the conference papers has taken a bit of time. The editors like to think that, with additional reflection on the proceedings in Bruges, the authors have managed to improve their papers measurably. We very much like to express our appreciation to all their efforts expended on the pages that follow. There is much in this volume that offers food for thought for the future.

Finally, we want to thank the sponsors of the conference, without whose support this whole exercise could not have taken place: the College of Europe, Bayer, European Generic Medicines Association, Evonik, Pernod Ricard, and the *Verband der Chemischen Industrie e. V.* (VCI).

Jacques Bourgeois   Marco Bronckers   Reinhard Quick

The Origins of WTO Dispute Settlement

Dirk De Bièvre[1]

1. Existing literature: on effects, rather than origins of WTO dispute settlement

The creation of the WTO dispute settlement system as a result of the Uruguay Round package has widely – and rightfully so – been regarded as an important development in international politics, international economic relations, and the evolution of multilateral institutions. Through the establishment World Trade Organization in 1995, the multilateral trade regime evolved from a typical case of intergovernmental international cooperation where states retain near-full control over decision to an institution where enforcement powers are partially delegated to third party bodies. During the preceding half century, dating back to the entry into force of the General Agreement on Tariffs and Trade (GATT) in 1948, the structure of reciprocal concessions in multilateral trade rounds had been the cornerstone of the multilateral trade regime. In the current international trade regime under the WTO however, reciprocal trade negotiations are not the only means through which WTO members can deal with existing barriers to trade among them. Members decided to strengthen existing mechanisms for enforcement of commonly agreed upon rules, replacing the GATT's model of political-diplomatic dispute settlement with a quasi-judicial model of dispute settlement characterized by automatic right to review, the formulation of legally binding obligations, a standing tribunal of justices, and the authority to authorize sanctions and even cross-retaliation against recalcitrant members (Goldstein *et al.* 2000; Stone Sweet 1997 and 1999; Zangl 2008).

Almost two decades have passed since the creation of the WTO dispute settlement mechanism (DSM). It has not been particularly surprising that scholarly attention for this institution has been large, one of the reasons being that this institutional innovation made the judicial pathway towards trade liberalization increasingly appealing to members of the trade regime, while the number of trade disputes increased dramatically (Weiler, 2001). While the vast majority of these

---

[1] Professor of international relations and international political economy, Department of Political Science and ACIM, Universiteit Antwerpen (<dirk.debievre@uantwerpen.be>).

disputes have not elicited compliance problems or significant public attention (Busch and Reinhardt, 2000, Wilson, 2007, Hudec, 1992), other disputes have been perceived to reach too deeply into practices of domestic governance and have thus become highly politicized, causing heated public debates at the domestic level and diplomatic tensions at the international level (Davis, 2003). Also, the legislative and judicial arms of the WTO have become increasingly intertwined as emerging economies have increasingly used litigation as a tool influence bargaining dynamics in the context of the multilateral trade negotiations, e.g. Doha round. More generally, the decline of the WTO as a forum for negotiated trade liberalization, epitomized by inability of the Doha Round to achieve substantive trade liberalization commitments, is further increasing the importance of the WTO's judicial arm as a tool to maintain a liberal trade regime (Irwin and Mavroidis, 2008).

Yet quite surprisingly, the literature about the origins of the WTO dispute settlement has been quite scant, sometimes flatly disappointing in its identification of systematic causes, constituting a gap in the political science literature that is only relatively recently being addressed. It is therefore my aim in this short contribution to the College of Europe colloquium on the WTO dispute settlement system to review and assess some of the existing explanations for the causes of the creation of the WTO dispute settlement mechanism, and to tentatively draw some inferences on the institution's actual function in contemporary trade relations.

2. The politics of WTO dispute settlement and identifying the key dimensions of international judicial institutions

After the creation of the WTO dispute settlement mechanism, a literature quickly developed on the so-called politics of WTO dispute settlement, i.e. on its effects on political behavior by states, their representatives, and to some lesser extent, the economic actors behind those. Importantly, this literature raised the awareness about the nature of the change that had occurred. Since it conceptualized which features of the trade regime had changed and had produced significant effects, it is useful to briefly review that literature, so as to identify which dimensions a good explanation of the very *creation* of the WTO DSM should be able to account for.

Scholars were quick to recognize that the reform of diplomatic GATT dispute settlement into the highly legalistic WTO dispute settlement formalized in 1995, constituted the most prominent step towards judicial institutions in the world trading regime. In the beginning of the eighties,

GATT contracting parties effectively abandoned the practice of vetoing GATT panel rulings (Hudec, 1992). In 1989, GATT contracting parties formally abolished the defendant's veto against the establishment of a panel in a decision that took immediate effect, independently from any further progress in the Uruguay Round negotiations going on at the same time (GATT, 1990). In 1994, all future members of the WTO approved of the Dispute Settlement Understanding that incorporated these two crucial changes, while adding yet two other crucial properties: the possibility of appeal with an independent and permanent WTO Appellate Body, and the possibility to have WTO panels authorize cross-retaliation by the complainant in cases of enduring non-compliance (WTO, 1995). By introducing the automatic right to review, the automatic adoption of legally binding rulings, a standing tribunal of justices, and the authority to authorize sanctions and even cross-retaliation against recalcitrant members, negotiators created one of the most judicialized global institutions, enabling it to significantly constrain the behavior of its constituent members towards respecting commonly agreed upon rules. This process of institutional transformation has commonly been captured with the term "legalization" (Abbott *et al.*, 2000, Goldstein *et al.*, 2000, Bernauer *et al.*, 2014), or "judicialization" (Zangl, 2008, Stone Sweet, 1997, Stone Sweet, 1999).

Both concepts denote an increased degree of enforceability of previously agreed upon rules. Yet, the use of the term legalization has generally been quite expansive, often resulting more in obfuscation than in clarification. The term legalization is generally used to cover the broad social phenomenon of an increase in the use of formal-legal rules to regulate a particular domain, *in casu* trade. It captures an increase in degree of precision, obligation, and bindingness, as well as an increase in enforceability through adjudication by an independent third party. The term judicialization, as introduced by Stone Sweet and usefully used by Zangl, refers more specifically to that latter aspect, namely the increase in enforceability through adjudication and authorization of sanctions by an independent third party. The terms legalization and judicialization are thus not entirely synonymous, but rather allow us to distinguish the broad process of subjecting trade matters to legally binding rules, from the ways in which judicial institutions affect the enforceability of those rules.

Rather than focusing on the causes of this judicialization of international interaction on trade matters, and thus on the origins of this strengthening of the enforcement mechanism for extant rules, the literature has primarily focused on its effects, focusing on a number of important aspects of the political-economy of WTO dispute settlement: the determinants of dispute initiation (Bernauer and Sattler, 2011, Busch *et al.*, 2009, Guzman and Simmons, 2005, Kim, 2008), strategic behavior by dispute settlement panels (Busch and Pelc, 2010, Garrett and Smith, 2002, Kelemen, 2001), the choice of institutional venue for resolving trade disputes (Davis and Shirato, 2007, Busch, 2007), why disputes escalate (Busch, 2000, Davis, 2012, Guzman and Simmons, 2002, Sattler and Bernauer, 2010), how litigation affects the domestic balance of trade-related interest groups (Goldstein and Martin, 2000, Goldstein and Steinberg, 2008) and under what conditions parties comply with decisions adopted through third party review (Bown, 2004, Davis, 2008). More generally, existing research shows that the judicialization of the WTO has brought about greater compliance with WTO rules (Zangl, 2008, Zangl *et al.*, 2011) and even acted as a buffer against protectionist policies being put into place in the very first place (Allee, 2005). Recent accounts of why the protectionist policies have not erupted as a result of the 2007-2008 financial crisis further stress this last point (Irwin and Mavroidis, 2008). This literature has certainly not reached its limits (for an overview, see De Bièvre and Poletti (2015) in a special issue of the *World Trade Review*). For instance, determining and measuring compliance is inherently difficult (it is private information to the litigating parties) and disentangling various potential causes for the policy change eventually leading to compliance requires an in-depth knowledge of the cases (Mavroidis, 2012), creating the classical conceptual dilemma of case sensitivity and the attempt to come to generalizable explanatory statements about variation among them. Also, research on the dynamics underlying the appointment of judges in WTO dispute settlement panels and the Appellate Body is still in its infancy (but see Elsig and Pollack, 2014). More research would also be welcome on the so-called non-cases, namely how litigants select cases out of the total universe of potential cases (Bernauer *et al.*, 2014).

3. Some problematic, seemingly self-evident explanations for the origin of WTO dispute settlement

Given the recognition that the creation of the WTO dispute settlement system was an important event in international politics, it is somewhat puzzling that so little research has been dedicated to explaining its causes. Moreover, explanations have tended to be posited *en passant*, as if the causes of its creation were entirely self-evident. As the following review of those will show, that is by no means the case. For one, many accounts fall prey to a functionalist fallacy, explaining the creation of the DSM with reference to the purposes it is supposedly fulfilling, for example allowing for efficient breach of rules under conditions of uncertainty (Downs and Rocke, 1995, Rosendorff, 2005, Schwartz and Sykes, 2002), filling contractual gaps between members of the regime (Horn *et al.*, 2010), or most obviously enhancing credibility of commitments by installing sanctioning devices against defection (Pelc, 2010). Functionalist accounts however, tend to employ explanations that merely establish that the observed outcome is consistent with the objectives the institutions were intended to reach. This type of explanation thus only weakly links the evidence adduced to the underlying causal mechanisms (Thompson, 2010). They also adopt a rather naïve conceptualization of power relations (whether symmetric or asymmetric) between key players that have the competence and power resources to instigate the institutional change, regardless of the aggregate outcome of this international cooperation to reform the institutions themselves. Moreover, functionalist approaches adopt a static view of actors' preferences, neglecting how past and new experiences, pre-existing institutional arrangements, and actors' interactions can affect those preferences and ultimately institutional design choices. More in particular, existing analyses often suffer from a US bias, considering motives of US policy makers as sufficient to explain this important international institutional process of reform, and neglecting how other important trade actors, in particular the EU, might have affected the negotiation processes leading to this particular design choice.

The most frustrating problem with the existing literature actually is therefore that it almost never addresses the question why WTO dispute settlement was created head-on. Instead, the topic is treated as if it was entirely clear why this happened, in order to then move on to a more specific question – a trait that is also very prominent in textbooks on international cooperation, international institutions, international economics, and/or international political economy.

So what are plausible reasons, origins, or causes for the institutional reform of the pre-existing GATT dispute settlement system?

The end of the Cold War? A first superficial candidate would seem that the end of the Cold War created the permissive conditions for a stronger belief by state representatives in the relevance and function of multilateral institutions. Generally popular among security-oriented international relations scholars, this explanation suffers from a couple of shortcomings. The GATT consisted primarily of the western, non-communist countries that had been located in the American camp of the Cold War military bipolarity. As a result, negotiations on the reform of GATT DS were entirely among those countries. The reform was negotiated between 1987 and 1993, and thus partly took place after the fall of the Berlin wall, yet any serious prospect of accession by China, let alone Russia, was to come far later.

Incrementalism? A second interpretation has been that the reform was some incremental, gradual move towards legalism and judicial decision-making – an autonomous, autopoietic development of a legal system beyond the control of member states. Popular among some lawyers and constructivist minded political scientists, this explanation is at odds with the jumps and starts in the development of both GATT and WTO dispute settlement. While the author of the bible on GATT dispute settlement, Robert Hudec has shown how the history of the GATT legal system consisted of dormant and activist periods (Hudec, 1992), some key aspects of the WTO DS reform like the guarantee of a right to a panel, the creation of the AB, and the elimination of the defendant's veto on the adoption of the panel and AB reports were discrete institutional changes that can hardly be conceived of as creeping or gradual.

Functionalism? One of the most standard textbook explanations of the WTO DSM is that it contributes to the solution of a prisoner's dilemma in international cooperation among states (Oatley, 2012). In game theory, a prisoner's dilemma arises when two players have similar preferences, but face uncertainty about the intentions of the other. Both realize that when each of them lowers its trade barriers, gains from cooperation will be forthcoming. Yet, the incentive to defect by keeping domestic market protection against foreign competition, while the other side duly opens its market, sabotages cooperation. This incentive can be particularly acute, if information about the actions and intentions about the other are scant. The other side opens up, you don't, and your pay-off is highest. This strategy dilemma – so the theory goes – can be overcome through iterated interaction and the application of reciprocity strategies (I respond with liberalization, if you liberalize; I respond with protection, if you play protect), as long as both sides keep caring about future benefits of cooperation. According to the application of the prisoner's dilemma metaphor to international trade cooperation, the succession of multilateral trade rounds builds the equivalent of iterated interaction, while the secretariat, the trade policy review mechanism, and the findings by panels and Appellate Body provide information on the behavior of other members. The more the dispute settlement system becomes independent from individual incentives to cheat, the better the institution is able to ensure an information-dense environment that forestalls cheating, or at least, forestalls a relapse from liberalize-liberalize, to protect-protect.

While the application of the prisoner's dilemma may be elucidating some aspects of the system once it was installed, it is hardly a plausible explanation for why states decided to forego the alleged benefits of cheating in the first place. In other words, a prisoner's dilemma theorization of WTO dispute settlement explains some of its effects, yet says precious little about how collective action on creating the institutional reform could produce this result. In short, such an explanation suffers from a functionalist fallacy.

For the same reason, the so-called rational design literature has remained largely silent about the origin of the creation of international judicial institutions, especially the strengthening of the GATT/WTO dispute settlement mechanism. Central in this literature is the tenet that uncertainty about the future distributional benefits of cooperation drives the design of institutions (Koremenos *et al.*, 2001). Yet, weirdly, this literature has shied away from offering a way in which such certainty or uncertainty may have encouraged or sabotaged the reform of the diplomatic GATT system into the judicial WTO procedure.

US hegemony? Prominent scholars have also maintained that the creation of the WTO dispute settlement can be explained by just focusing on the motives of one member of the world trading system, the United States, by positing that the US had a desire to increase the legitimacy of the system (Goldstein and Gowa, 2002, Goldstein, 1998). Such explanations thus actually take it for granted that a mono-causal explanation can provide a necessary and sufficient condition for this reform to take place. Looked at it from a domestic US perspective, this view has a certain merit. The US Trade Representative's office found itself in a strong bargaining position as it could regularly point out how a recalcitrant Congress narrowed its margin for maneuver in letting other states not respect international law commitments entered into with the US. While thus voicing the interests of offensive, market opening interests in the US legislature, Congress equally made itself available for defensive, market protection voices by trying to display its purported superiority over supranational institutions by making approval of the WTO Dispute Settlement Mechanism conditional upon a report whether rulings of the WTO DSB would be in accordance with US preferences (Horlick, 1995). This concession by the Clinton administration to these defensive voices turned out to be a null and void threat as it was never acted upon in the years that were to follow.

While attractive in its simplicity, the US hegemony explanation is at odds with quite substantial empirics. First, the suggestion that the GATT had been the product of US hegemony actually has far less empirical basis than would seem on the basis of the standard international law and economics literature, since the GATT only started to serve a role as forum for drastic liberalization commitments after the creation of the European Community, as American exporters mobilized to claw back some of their lost market shares (Dür, 2010, De Bièvre and Poletti, 2013). It was exactly this threat of market share that caused the US to have to negotiate from a position of relative weakness, as the European side could often wait and see, and ask for counter concessions beneficial to European exporters. Second, while the US aggressive unilateral strategy of trying to punish US trading partners through the use of its Section 301 investigations and the threat with, or the actual imposition of trade sanctions, the success of these actions was relatively modest (Bayard and Elliott, 1994). More specifically however, the US opposed and only recalcitrantly accepted the creation of the WTO Appellate Body, tried and failed to maintain its sovereign right to determine itself when market access commitments had been fulfilled and thus lost its autonomy to determine itself when it wanted to impose retaliatory measures (Hudec, 2000).

The explanation thus lies all but with an alleged hegemonic power preponderance of only one of the near 150 GATT contracting parties. Numerous accounts of the outcomes and processes of the Uruguay Round have concurred in the observation of a near symmetrical power relationship between the two key powers, the EU and the US, involved in these negotiations limited to the issue area of trade. Although legally and formally wed to the principle of one member one vote, the membership of the GATT and the early WTO years was prone to striking power asymmetries in favor of the tandem driven by the European Union and the United States. This effectively meant that any deal between these two on substantive as well as procedural issues was a near done deal for all the membership, especially when the EU and the US could threaten to declare their own GATT market access commitments null and void for those states that would not want to join the WTO (Steinberg, 2002).

So what is left? Of course, in some sense my above juxtaposition of failing attempts to try and explain the creation of strong judicial institutions in the world trade regime does injustice to all of them. Indeed, theoretically coherent explanations are intended to provide explanations for events of the same kind. Yet, exactly the seeming uniqueness of the event creates the challenge of coming to a plausible theoretical account of this remarkable institutional development.

4. Bilateral EU – US bargaining and a multilateral outcome

In a special issue of the *World Trade Review* on "Judicial institutions in international trade relations" (De Bièvre and Poletti, 2015), Manfred Elsig and Jappe Eckhardt from the World Trade Institute in Bern, explain how previous experience with the GATT DS system informed EU and US negotiators about what their chances of success and failure in a strengthened dispute mechanism might look like (Elsig and Eckhardt, 2015). In doing so, they give further credence to the basic argument made by Hudec in one of his last contributions, namely that the iterated interaction between US unilateralism and EU recalcitrance provided the essential building blocks for a deal in which each side received a trophy (Hudec, 2000). At the initial stage, the two large GATT members US and EU seemed diametrically opposed in this negotiation. The EC did not want to see a move toward automaticity and the elimination of multiple veto points in the entire procedure for fear that several of its policies, not least its agricultural policy, would face death by a thousand cuts. The EC defended this position with reference to the importance of consensus, arbitration and the like. On the other hand, the US – although sometimes wrongly characterized as inherently having more of a legal culture of adversarial legalism than other legal systems – did not propose and was certainly not supportive of the creation of an appeals court (probably the reason why the institution in the end acquired the incredibly ugly and un-English name of "Appellate Body").

Yet, the end result turned out to be exactly a combination of those two elements that characterize the move to judicialization identified earlier in this report. The puzzle of the creation of the WTO dispute settlement indeed seems double. What needs explaining are the acquiescence with automaticity throughout the procedure on the part of the EC, and the acquiescence with the creation of the AB and the delegation of powers to determine the right to retaliate on the part of the US. Elsig and Eckhardt show that the US was motivated by its experience of mostly winning its cases, regularly forcing complainants against it into withdrawal, and managing not to implement when it was itself on the losing side. As for the EC, these experiences were quite different, as it was not very good at winning cases it brought, had a mixed record in defending itself, and regularly failed to implement. After what must have been a good row within the Commission over how to deal with non-violation cases, more law experts were put in charge so that the insight that non-violation cases should and could actually be won took root. Furthermore, the EC acted as the *porte-parole* of those GATT members that were extremely concerned about the negative externalities of US unilateral retaliation policies under the Section 301 procedure.

The self-perception of benefiting from the system enabled the US to take a bold stance and risk a strengthening of the system through the introduction of automaticity, while accepting a "multilateralization" of the authorization of sanctions in cases of non-compliance. The EC by contrast, was happy to get the prize of taking the decision on sanctions out of the hands of individual WTO members, especially out of the hands of the USTR, and put its hopes in the legal check by an appeals instance.

5. Implications for the actual functioning of the WTO Dispute Settlement Mechanism

Such an explanation, simple as it might look, works with a couple of implicit statements that are indeed different from those sometimes used in the other explanations reviewed above.

First, it was a deal between equals, and not the result of alleged US hegemony. Both the EU and the US had the power resources to insist on getting some of their preferences realized, whereas none of them was able to get the whole prize of only its own preferences fulfilled. Hegemonic phantasies may have informed US attempts at legitimating existing practice, yet declaratory politics is not implementation politics.

Second, interaction was not just an autonomous development of legal practice, away from the influence of state power. Delegation of particular powers was a deliberate act of EU and US negotiators trying to maximize what they could carry home to their capitals.

Third, the reform seems to have been relatively little caused by a purported motive to strengthen incentives against "cheating" upon previous commitments. The basic deal about strengthening of the dispute settlement mechanism, consisting of the 1989 reform and the early negotiating deal on the AB in 1993 may well have emboldened negotiators on other elements of the WTO package to dare and enter into commitments that would require serious surveillance and implementation issues, such as the TRIPS, TBT or SPS agreements. Yet, this again is a possible *effect*, rather than a cause of the move towards judicial procedure.

Fourth, the motivation to create equal opportunities for all GATT and future WTO members played no role during the negotiation process, whereas the purported advantages to smaller and weaker member states were actively trumpeted in order to legitimize the new procedures *post factum*. Not surprisingly, equality among members in dispute settlement did increase, yet did not eliminate the inherent weaker position of smaller and less developed countries, because of their smaller legal capacity, their lesser degree of economic diversification or right away oligopolistic economic structure, and their ensuing weaker domestic interest representation systems (Bown, 2009, Shaffer and Melendez-Ortiz, 2010).

References

ABBOTT, K. W., KEOHANE, R. O., MORAVCSIK, A., SLAUGHTER, A.-M. & SNIDAL, D. 2000. The Concept of Legalization. *International Organization*, 54, 401-419.

ALLEE, T. 2005. The "Hidden" Impact of the World Trade Organization on the Reduction of Trade Conflict. *2005 Midwest Political Science Association Conference*. Chicago, Illinois.

BAYARD, T. O. & ELLIOTT, K. A. 1994. *Reciprocity and retaliation in U.S. trade policy*, Washington DC, Institute for international economics.

BERNAUER, T., ELSIG, M. & PAUWELYN, J. 2014. Dispute Settlement Mechanism: Analysis and Problems. In DAUNTON, M., NARLIKAR, A. & STERN, R. M. (eds.) *The Oxford Handbook on The World Trade Organization* Oxford: Oxford University Press.

BERNAUER, T. & SATTLER, T. 2011. Gravitation or discrimination? Determinants of litigation in the World Trade Organization. *European Journal of Political Research*, 50, 143-167.

BOWN, C. 2004. On the Economic Success of GATT/WTO Dispute Settlement. *The Review of Economics and Statistics*, 86, 811-823.

BOWN, C. 2009. *Self Enforcing Trade*, Washington, Brookings.

BUSCH, M. L. 2000. Democracy, Consultation, and the Paneling of Disputes Under GATT. *Journal of Conflict Resolution*, 44, 425-46.

BUSCH, M. L. 2007. Overlapping Institutions, Forum Shopping, and Dispute Settlement in International Trade. *International Organization*, 61, 735-761.

BUSCH, M. L. & PELC, K. J. 2010. The Politics of Judicial Economy at the World Trade Organization. *International Organization*, 64, 257-279.

BUSCH, M. L. & REINHARDT, E. 2000. Bargaining in the Shadow of the Law: Early Settlement in GATT/WTO Disputes, *Fordham International Law Journal*, 24, 158-172.

BUSCH, M. L., REINHARDT, E. & SHAFFER, G. 2009. Does legal capacity matter? A survey of WTO Members. *World Trade Review*, 8, 559-577.

DAVIS, C. J. 2003. *Food Fights Over Free Trade: How International Institutions and Issue Linkage Promote Agricultural Trade Liberalization*, Princeton, Princeton University Press.

DAVIS, C. J. 2008. The Effectiveness of WTO Dispute Settlement: an Evaluation of Negotiations versus Adjudication Strategies. *Annual Meeting of the American Political Science Association.* Boston.

DAVIS, C. J. 2012. *Why adjudicate? Enforcing Trade Rules in the WTO*, Princeton, Princeton University Press.

DAVIS, C. J. & SHIRATO, Y. 2007. Firms, governments, and WTO adjudication: Japan's selection of WTO disputes. *World Politics*, 59, 274-313.

DE BIEVRE, D. & POLETTI, A. 2015. Judicial Politics in International Trade Relations, introduction to the special issue. *World Trade Review*, S.1-11.

DE BIÈVRE, D. & POLETTI, A. 2013. The EU in EU trade policy. From regime shaper to status quo power. In FALKNER, G. & MÜLLER, P. (eds.) *EU Policies in a Global Perspective.* London: Routledge.

DOWNS, G. W. & ROCKE, D. M. 1995. *Optimal Imperfection? Domestic Uncertainty and Institutions in International Relations*, Princeton, Princeton University Press.

DÜR, A. 2010. *Protection for Exporters. Power and Discrimination in Transatlantic Trade Relations, 1930-2010*, Ithaca and London, Cornell University Press.

ELSIG, M. & ECKHARDT, J. 2015. The Creation of the Multilateral Trade Court: Design and Experiential Learning. *World Trade Review*, S.13-32.

ELSIG, M. & POLLACK, M. A. 2014. Agents, trustees, and international courts: The politics of judicial appointment at the World Trade Organization. *European Journal of International Relations*, 20, 391-415.

GARRETT, G. & SMITH, J. M. 2002. *The politics of WTO dispute settlement. UCLA Occasional Papers Series.*

GATT 1990. Improvements to the GATT Dispute Settlement Rules and Procedures, Decision of 12 April 1989 (L/6489). In GATT, T. C. P. T. T. (ed.) *Basic Instruments and Selected Documents, Thirty-sixth Supplement. Protocols, Decisions, Reports 1988-1989 and Forty-fifth Session.* Geneva: GATT.

GOLDSTEIN, J. & GOWA, J. 2002. US national power and the post-war trading regime. *World Trade Review*, 1, 153-170.

GOLDSTEIN, J., KAHLER, M., KEOHANE, R. & SLAUGHTER, A.-M. 2000. Introduction: Legalization and World Politics. *International Organization*, 54, 385-399.

GOLDSTEIN, J. J. & STEINBERG, R. R. 2008. Negotiate or litigate? Effects of WTO judicial delegation on US trade politics. *Law and Contemporary Problems*, 71, 257-82.

GOLDSTEIN, J. L. 1998. International institutions and domestic policies: GATT, WTO, and the liberalization of international trade. In KRUEGER, A. O. (ed.) *The WTO as an international organization.* Chicago: Chicago University Press.

GOLDSTEIN, J. L. & MARTIN, L. L. 2000. Legalization, Trade Liberalization, and Domestic Politics: A Cautionary Note. *International Organization*, 54, 603-632.

GUZMAN, A. T. & SIMMONS, B. A. 2002. To Settle or Empanel? An Empirical Analysis of Litigation and Settlement at the WTO. *Journal of Legal Studies*, 31, 205-227.

GUZMAN, A. T. & SIMMONS, B. A. 2005. Power Plays and Capacity Constraints: The Selection of Defendants in WTO Disputes. *Journal of Legal Studies*, 34, 557-98.

HORLICK, G. N. 1995. WTO Dispute Settlement and the Dole Commission. *Journal of World Trade*, 29, 45-48.

HORN, H., MAGGI, G. & STAIGER, R. W. 2010. Trade Agreements as Endogenously Incomplete Contracts. *American Economic Review*, 100, 394-419.

HUDEC, R. E. 1992. *Enforcing international trade law: the evolution of the modern GATT legal system,* Salem, N.H., Butterworth.

HUDEC, R. E. 2000. Broadening the scope of remedies in WTO dispute settlement. In WEISS, F. (ed.) *Improving WTO dispute settlement procedures – Issues and lessons from the practice of other international courts and tribunals.* London: Cameron May.

IRWIN, D. A. & MAVROIDIS, P. C. 2008. The WTO's Difficulties in Light of the GATT's History. *Vox.*

KELEMEN, R. D. 2001. The limits of judicial power: trade-environment disputes in the GATT/WTO and the EU. *Comparative Political Studies*, 34, 622-650.

KIM, M. 2008. Costly Procedures: Divergent Effects of Legalization in the GATT/WTO Dispute Settlement Procedures. *International Studies Quarterly*, 52, 657-686.

KOREMENOS, B., LIPSON, C. & SNIDAL, D. 2001. The Rational Design of International Institutions. *International Organization*, 55, 761-799.

MAVROIDIS, P. C. 2012. On compliance in the WTO: enforcement among unequal disputants. *Briefing Paper*. Geneva: CUTS International.

OATLEY, T. 2012. *International Political Economy: Interests and Institutions in the Global Economy*, New York, Longman.

PELC, K. J. 2010. Eluding efficiency: why do we not see more efficient breach at the WTO? *World Trade Review*, 9, 629-642.

ROSENDORFF, P. B. 2005. Stability and Rigidity: Politics and Design of the WTO's Dispute Settlement Procedure. *American Political Science Review*, 99.

SATTLER, T. & BERNAUER, T. 2010. Gravitation or discrimination? Determinants of litigation in the World Trade Organisation. *European Journal of Political Research*, 143-167.

SCHWARTZ, W. & SYKES, A. O. 2002. The Economic Structure of Renegotiation and Dispute Resolution in the World Trade Organization. *Journal of Legal Studies*, 31, 179-204.

SHAFFER, G. & MELENDEZ-ORTIZ, R. (eds.) 2010. *Dispute Settlement at the WTO: The Developing Country Experience*, Cambridge: Cambridge University Press.

STEINBERG, R. 2002. In the Shadow of Law or Power? Consensus-Based Bargaining and Outcomes in the GATT/WTO. *International Organization*, 56, 339-374.

STONE SWEET, A. 1997. The New GATT: Dispute resolution and the judicialisation of the trade regime. In VOLCANSEK, M. L. (ed.) *Law Above Nations: Supranational Courts and the Legalization of Politics*. Gainesville: University Press of Florida.

STONE SWEET, A. 1999. Judicialization and the construction of governance. *Comparative Political Studies*, 32, 147-184.

THOMPSON, A. 2010. Rational design in motion: Uncertainty and flexibility in the global climate regime. *European Journal of International Relations*, 16, 269-296.

WEILER, J. H. H. 2001. The Rule of Lawyers and the Ethos of Diplomats: Reflections on the Internal and External Legitimacy of WTO Dispute Settlement. *Journal of World Trade*, 35, 191-207.

WILSON, B. 2007. Compliance by WTO Members with Adverse WTO Dispute Settlement Rulings: The Record to Date. *Journal of International Economic Law*, 10, 397-403.

WTO 1995. *The WTO dispute settlement procedures: a collection of legal texts*, Geneva, World Trade Organization.

ZANGL, B. 2008. Judicialization Matters! A Comparison of Dispute Settlement Under GATT and the WTO. *International Studies Quarterly*, 52, 825-854.

ZANGL, B., HELMEDACH, A., MONDRÉ, A., KOCKS, A., NEUBAUER, G. & BLOME, K. 2011. Between law and politics: Explaining international dispute settlement behavior. *European Journal of International Relations*.

A Comment

Lothar EHRING[1]

I will come back to the origin of the dispute settlement system at the end, but I will start in the present and make a few remarks about certain features of the dispute settlement system today. We face today a dispute settlement system of the WTO that is highly effective, but lives in an era of dysfunctional negotiations at the WTO, thus creating an imbalance of powers and a deficiency in terms of adaptations of the law, also in response to judicial rulings, where considered necessary. Claus Ehlermann has just made the point that this is an important problem, the point is being made in many places, he and I even jointly made it in one publication. Nevertheless, this does not mean that it is not worth calling into question the validity of this proposition. One can easily explain politically that the imbalance and lack of legislative response are a problem. But whether it is really a danger in the long term for the WTO, I think, is a question that needs to be measured against the yard-stick of the reality today, where we have a very well-functioning WTO dispute settlement system which for unfortunately already many years lives next to a negotiation forum in the WTO that is inoperable and certainly ineffective, when it comes to results.

This admittedly creates problems of an institutional nature for instance inside the WTO Secretariat where the work is unevenly distributed between those who would ideally service negotiations and those who deal with dispute settlement and are fully stretched or over-stretched. But whether the imbalance is a problem also outside the institution of the Secretariat, notably for the Membership, I think, has to be turned against the WTO Members themselves whose choice it is collectively that things be as they are. The WTO Members are all entitled to be dissatisfied with the situation in the sense that they would like a functional negotiation forum and I certainly would support that myself. But collectively the Members are the ones who are responsible for it not to work and they seem relatively happy with the fact that the dispute settlement system is working well, really well, maybe better than ever before. If you look at the jurisprudence of the last three to five years, you find there major

---

[1]   Assessor Iuris, M.P.A. (Harvard); Official of the European Commission, expressing only personal views which should not be regarded as representing the view of the European Commission.

decisions that are extremely well reasoned, on extremely important and difficult interpretative questions. These questions were disposed of in a remarkable manner, convincingly and also accepted by the Membership which comes back for more, with more cases.

Thus, provocatively, I would respond: is there really such a big problem for the dispute settlement system itself? Of course, for the WTO as a whole the picture is different. We have also seen that the absence of success in negotiations can lead to the use of alternatives in certain narrow areas where you can push the development of the law through litigation. Notably, in the area of dispute settlement procedures, optional open hearings, that is public access to hearings of panels and the Appellate Body, became possible in the practice as a result of litigation efforts of individual WTO Members which pushed for a more innovative interpretation of the existing rules. In the negotiation room, despite heavy efforts over many years, open hearings remained unachievable even in an optional mode where every Member could have opposed it in individual cases. There is also a negative example I want to give on the choice between litigation and negotiation as tools for the achievement of an objective: remember how, in the early stages of the Doha Round, Brazil brought the cotton dispute, and lobbied for the participation of African countries who could have participated as co-complainants at zero cost? They declined and instead opted for pursuing their objectives in the negotiation framework, without success. More than ten years later, the cotton aspect is still part of the unfished or perhaps unfinishable business of the Doha Agenda. In the future, governments should factor in their past experience and realistically evaluate the prospects of getting something tricky done in negotiations.

My second point is about dispute settlement in an era of protectionism. As you may know, there are two versions on the state of protectionism: there is the public version of the WTO and WTO Members as well as in academia, based on research, that there has been no surge, or no major, significant surge of protectionism since the crisis, since 2009 roughly speaking. At the same time, there is monitoring, and the WTO has ably occupied the field by participating in this monitoring. Much less successful, however, is the follow up regarding the protectionist measures identified. If you look at the numbers of this reporting, there is protectionism all around the world and there are very problematic phenomena: most notably, I would mention local content requirements that are mushrooming around the world, and there seems to exist little of a strategy in the WTO on how to go after them effectively. In my personal view, the best way to go after local content requirements is to litigate against them immediately because they have very rapid dynamic effects of attracting investments which cannot and will not be rolled back even if five years later a WTO dispute concludes and the measure is removed. And just to give you an example of the sometimes political nature of the presentation: in June 2014 the WTO Director-General Azevêdo issued a statement that trade restrictions were "down slightly", this was the subject line of the notice which disseminated the WTO report on the G-20 members' trade measures. The reality (expressed in the body of the message) was that 112 *new* restrictive measures had been adopted in six months, compared to 115 new measures in the previous six months. Of course, that was a few down but only in the *rate of increase* and therefore still an addition to the stock of existing restrictive measures because we all know that most of the 115 new measures of the previous semester probably were still in force. He concluded that the WTO must "remain watchful", which is of course fine but not alone a matter of counting restrictive measures as they accumulate and do not disappear.

My third point is about the dispute settlement system in an era of bilateralism. Claus Ehlermann has entered in to that subject as well. Is it a risk for the WTO? Empirically not because WTO Members do not use these bilateral dispute settlement systems so far. They prefer to keep submitting their disputes to the WTO, and this for very good reasons – I would do exactly the same. Except, of course, if this is not possible, notably if you want to enforce pure WTO-plus, where you may have no alternative to bilateral dispute settlement. This afternoon there is a session that should deepen that aspect and perhaps I can comment there on why I think, contrary to Claus Ehlermann, that it would be not just unlikely but even undesirable to integrate FTA dispute settlement into the WTO.

My final point is about WTO dispute settlement in an era of fundamental controversy. By fundamental controversy I mean the partial dissatisfaction that the WTO Member to which the WTO's dispute settlement system is largely owed has been expressing for over ten years now in relation to the functioning of the dispute settlement system. This WTO Member was by the way not just the main driver behind the creation of the dispute settlement system, not just in the Uruguay Round, but even beforehand when the Legal Office of the GATT Secretariat was created. This is something that we owe to this WTO Member first and foremost. They were the ones who wanted legalization, they were the ones who wanted stronger enforcement, they were the ones who wanted legal principles to be applied in GATT dispute settlement, and the others at some point were ready to follow. It is very valuable to remember that when over the last good ten years we have seen a certain degree of unhappiness of the same Member, including the criticism that the Appellate Body has breached the ban on adding obligations and diminishing rights. You can find an excellent account of that perspective in a recent publication by Terence Stewart and others in the Global Trade and Customs Journal with the title "The Increasing Recognition of Problems with WTO Appellate Body Decision-Making". It is about little more than this whole proposition that the adjudicators in Geneva are filling gaps. The biggest disappointment in this debate in my eyes is the lack of recognition by those critics that this is all a matter of subjective perception. One Member's gap that it does not want to be filled, is another Member's right which it does not get enforced, because at the end of the day they just disagree over whether there is a gap. If one Member considers that there is a gap in the rules and the measure allowed, but the other Member believes that there is an obligation that is breached, then this disagreement has to be resolved multilaterally by an independent institution. In the WTO we have such independent institutions, it is the Appellate Body as the last resort. It obviously cannot be individual Members who have the final word on what is the correct interpretation of the WTO Agreement. This has to be independent institutions even if those who have the final word may make mistakes. All human institutions make mistakes; if we were part of those institutions, then we too would make mistakes. I certainly would make more mistakes than these people who are in office are making.

Of course, we each have our own list of things we think the Appellate Body has not ruled 100% convincingly. I could give you my list, it is a short list, but still it exists. But that does not detract from the necessity to have an independent institution that makes the final ruling which all the subjects of the legal order in question must accept, no matter whether they would have decided in the same way. So it is essential to have an independent institution that decides bindingly for everybody what is the correct interpretations of WTO law. If this job is done so remarkably well as it is by the Appellate Body, then there is no good reason to be dissatisfied. Interestingly, one can look at individual cases in which the Member in question requested and happily obtained from the Appellate Body interpretations which one could, if one wanted and from the opposite perspective, describe as gap filling. For example the decision that oral hearings of the Appellate Body can be open to the public or the correction of the drafting mistake of Article 2.1 of the TBT Agreement, by reading into it the possibility of justification. Please do not get me wrong: in my view, these are excellent decisions and they are legally correct, very convincing and can count as masterpieces of the Appellate Body's work. However, those who had or have the opposite opinion, can find ways to argue that they represent gap filling.

Jurisdiction and Applicable Law in the WTO

Lorand BARTELS[1]

1. Introduction

This chapter considers the law applicable by WTO panels and the Appellate Body in dispute settlement proceedings. It begins by explaining how law is applied to facts, and how this is relevant to the exercise of jurisdiction by WTO panels and the Appellate Body. It then looks at several discrete sets of legal questions, both jurisdictional and merits, in which questions related to applicable law arise.

The jurisdictional questions, broadly speaking, that are considered concern the power of panels to determine the legality of their establishment, the power of panels to determine whether other preconditions to the exercise of their jurisdiction have been met, including what is elsewhere termed "admissibility". The merits questions concern the law applicable to the proper identification of the facts and to the law applicable to these facts, based on the various overlapping provisions in the DSU pertaining to these matters, and taking into account the possible role of non-WTO law.

In addressing these questions, this chapter adopts a quite particular understanding of the legal process by which rules are applied to facts. In brief, this understanding is that every legal rule is based on a description of certain hypothetical facts and can be applied to any given "fact", no matter how remote it might appear to be to the facts described in the rule, and the result will necessarily generate a binary outcome. Either the "fact" falls within the set of "facts" described by the rule, or it will not. There is no third option.[2]

It is important to distinguish this sense of rule application from a second sense, in which a rule is said to "apply" to a given "fact" when it is *relevant* to that fact. Actually, what this second sense of the word "apply" means is

---

[1]   University of Cambridge. Email: <lab53@cam.ac.uk>. This paper was presented at a Colloquium on WTO law at the College of Europe, Bruges on 12 September 2014. I am grateful for comments by the participants in the conference, in particular Mary Footer and Jan Bohanes, and also Michelle Zhang.

[2]   This process is usually called "subsumption". See Robert Alexy, "On Balancing and Subsumption: A Structural Comparison"(2003) 15 Ratio Juris 433, 435; Neil MacCormick, *Legal Reasoning and Legal Theory* (Oxford: OUP, 1994), passim, and Frederick Schauer, "Formalism" (1988) 97 Yale Law Journal 509, at 534.

that the "fact" has a reasonable prospect of falling within the set of facts described by the rule. Thus, on this second meaning, one might say that a rule about vehicles does not "apply" to dogs, because there is no chance that a dog might be a vehicle, whereas it might "apply" to skateboards or tanks on plinths.[3] Both senses follow normal linguistic usage.[4] However, it can also be seen that this second sense of "apply" is no more than an informal means of saying that there is a very low probability, perhaps even zero, that a rule will "apply" to a fact in the first sense of the word "apply". Essentially, this prejudges the issue. After all, one cannot *ex ante* exclude the possibility that a dog might be a vehicle too.

A second preliminary point should also be made, concerning the nature of "facts" for the purpose of a rule-fact relationship. The view is adopted here that, for this purpose, "facts" can include not only "brute facts", such as things or conduct,[5] but also "institutional facts",[6] such as rules, or legal determinations. At a greater level of abstraction, one can conceive of "facts" for these purposes as the minor term in any legal formula (whether, for definitional facts, this is in the form of a syllogism or whether, for rules setting out a legal consequence, this is in the form of an "if-then" propositional formula) in which the major term is the rule, and the conclusion is a binary legal outcome that depends on whether the "fact" at issue is within the set of hypothetical "facts" described in the rule.

Third, it is assumed in this chapter that the question whether, and how, a panel or the Appellate Body applies rules to facts is properly seen in terms of their jurisdictional powers. Nonetheless, certain distinctions can be drawn. First, panel and the Appellate Body applies primary rules to "facts" when this is the primary question before them, and for this purpose primary questions may be jurisdictional or merits based.[7] Second, it is

---

3   This is to be distinguished from the question whether a given *legal system* says anything about a given fact. It is possible to say that a legal system is neutral with respect to the fact, on which cf. the Declaration of Judge Simma in *Kosovo (Advisory Opinion)* [2010] ICJ Rep 403, paras 1-3 and 9. In a concrete sense, though, if a legal system is neutral, the "fact" at issue will be irrelevant (for definitional rules) or permitted (for rules with a legal consequence), by operation of the liberal default principle, common to all legal systems, and reflected in *Lotus (France v Turkey)* [1927] PCIJ (Ser A) No 10, at 18-19, that, except for public authorities limited by the principle of conferred powers, what is not expressly prohibited is permitted. For this as a principle of English constitutional law, see John Laws, "The Rule of Reason – An International Heritage" in Mad Andenas and Duncan Fairgrieve (eds.), *Judicial Review in International Perspective* (The Hague: Kluwer, 2000) at 256. For a recent sensible reading of *Lotus* see An Hertogen, "Letting *Lotus* Bloom" (2015) 26 EJIL 901.

4   Definitions 6(a) and 6(b) of "apply" in *Oxford English Dictionary*, 3rd ed. (Oxford: OUP, 2008).

5   G E M Anscombe, "On Brute Facts" (1958) 18 Analysis 69.

6   Neil McCormick, "Law as Institutional Fact" (1974) 90 LQR 102.

7   Lorand Bartels, "Jurisdiction and Applicable Law Clauses in International Law: Where Does a Tribunal Find the Principal Norms Applicable to the Case Before It?" in Tomer Broude and Yuval Shany (eds.), *Multi-Sourced Equivalent Norms in*

necessary, subject to any contrary applicable rule, to determine whether a given primary rule is applicable, and this question is determined by applying relevant rules on the applicability of that primary rule, which is to say, a "metanorm", to that primary rule (which functions as a "fact" for this purpose).[8] Third, legal "facts" are often, though not necessarily, established by reference to the legal conclusions resulting from the application of other rules, including rules from other legal systems, to a given "fact", which may be of a different nature.

The following illustrates the implications of this approach to applicable law in terms of questions of the jurisdiction of WTO panels and the Appellate Body. The key questions in each case concern the identification of the primary "law" that is to be applied to the "facts" at issue, the "law" that determines whether and, if so, how that primary "law" can be applied to those "facts" in the case at hand, how "facts" with a legal dimension are to be ascertained, and the power of WTO panels and the Appellate Body and (where relevant) the Dispute Settlement Body, to deal with these issues.

2. Jurisdictional questions

2.1 Introduction

At the jurisdictional stage, broadly speaking, applicable law issues arise in relation to questions concerning the proper establishment of a panel, questions concerning the satisfaction of any preconditions – whether set out in WTO law or otherwise – that must be satisfied before a panel or the Appellate Body can exercise jurisdiction, and questions concerning the substance of any questions arising before panels and the Appellate Body. An initial question concerns the scope of a panel's (or the Appellate Body's) *compétence de la competence* to determine such questions. As the ICJ said in *Nottebohm*, every international tribunal has "the right to decide as to its own jurisdiction".[9] For its part, the Appellate Body has confirmed that it applies the same principle applies in WTO law.[10]

International Law (Oxford: Hart, 2011), discussed in *Application of the Genocide Convention (Croatia v Serbia)* [2015] ICJ Rep nyr, Judge ad hoc Kreća, Separate Opinion, paras 69-73.

8   Bartels, *ibid.*, and Judge ad hoc Kreća, Separate Opinion, *ibid.*

9   *Nottebohm (Liechtenstein v Guatemala)*, Preliminary Objection [1953] ICJ Rep 111, at 119.

10   WTO panels have this power: WTO Appellate Body Report, *US – 1916 Act*, WT/DS136/AB/R, adopted 26 September 2000, at para. 54, n 30 (noting that "a widely accepted rule that an international tribunal is entitled to consider the issue of its own jurisdiction on its own initiative, and to satisfy itself that it has jurisdiction in any case that comes before it") and WTO Appellate Body Report, *Mexico – Corn*

However, the ICJ added that this is "in the absence of any agreement to the contrary".[11] Moreover, there are other reasons why a panel or the Appellate Body might not be able to determine such questions.

2.2 Proper establishment of a panel

WTO panels are established by a decision of the Dispute Settlement Body under Article 6.1 DSU.[12] This raises the question whether a panel is competent to review that decision.

The Appellate Body has said that "[a]s a panel request is normally not subjected to detailed scrutiny by the DSB, it is incumbent upon a panel to examine the request for the establishment of the panel very carefully to ensure its compliance with both the letter and the spirit of Article 6.2 of the DSU".[13] But this rather broad statement must be qualified. Formally speaking, if a panel request does not comply with the conditions set out in Article 6.2, the result is that the DSB's decision to establish a panel under Article 6.1 is *ultra vires*. What the Appellate Body must have meant is that a panel must confine its terms of reference, established under Article 7, to legal claims and measures set out in a valid panel request under Article 6.2. The Appellate Body put the matter more accurately in *EC – Certain Customs Matters* when it said:

> Pursuant to Article 7.1 of the DSU, a panel's terms of reference are governed by the request for the establishment of a panel. In other words, the panel request identifies the measures and the claims that a panel will have the authority to examine and on which it will have the authority to make findings.[14]

But this still does not answer the question whether a panel may consider the legality of the DSB decision under Article 6.1 under which it is established. As foreshadowed, there is a good reason why panels should not have such a power. This is because of the logical paradox that a panel that is not properly established cannot determine anything, including whether it was properly or improperly established, while a panel that *is* properly established cannot logically determine that it *not* is properly established.[15]

Syrup (Art 21.5 – US), WT/DS132/AB/RW, adopted 21 November 2001, para. 36. It follows from the Appellate Body's statement in *US – 1916 Act* that the Appellate Body has this power too.

[11] *Nottebohm*, above at n 9.

[12] All subsequent references to treaty provisions are to the DSU unless otherwise stated.

[13] WTO Appellate Body Report, *EC – Bananas III*, WT/DS27/AB/R, adopted 25 September 1997, para. 142.

[14] WTO Appellate Body Report, *EC – Certain Customs Matters*, WT/DS315/AB/R, adopted 11 December 2006, para. 131.

[15] Mohamed Shahabuddeen, *International Criminal Justice at the Yugoslav Tribunal* (Oxford: OUP, 2012), at 58-61. Tayyab Mahmud, "Praetorianism and Common

Hence, logically speaking, a panel enquiring into whether it is properly established is only able to determine that it is properly established, which is a predetermined result. In short, a panel *can* entertain the question whether it is properly established, but because the result of such a question is predetermined, it *should not* entertain this question.

It might be objected that a panel must have a separate jurisdiction to consider whether it is properly established, just as international commercial arbitration tribunals typically have the power to determine the legality of their establishment. However, in theoretical terms, these tribunals only have such a power because they are ultimately governed by a supervening legal system capable of authorizing such a power.[16] This is quite different in international law, as it is for superior domestic courts.[17] So, for instance, ICSID tribunals have no power to consider whether the decision of the ICSID Secretary-General to register a request for arbitration is valid,[18] and, despite some decisions to the contrary, at least some international criminal tribunals have come to the same conclusion.[19]

The same view has been taken in WTO jurisprudence. In *Australia – Automotive Leather* Australia argued that a panel was improperly

---

Law in Post-Colonial Settings: Judicial Responses to Constitutional Breakdowns in Pakistan" (1993) Utah L Rev 1225, at 1301 takes the view that constitutional courts are permitted to determine such questions on the basis of "extra-constitutional powers" justified on the grounds of "state necessity". This view is criticized by Simeon McIntosh, *Kelsen in the "Grenada Court": Essays on Revolutionary Legality* (Kingston: Ian Randle, 2008) at 151-156.

[16] Emmanuel Gaillard and John Savage (eds.), *Fouchard, Gaillard, Goldman on International Commercial Arbitration* (The Hague: Kluwer, 1999), at 400: "[H]ow can an arbitrator, solely on the basis of an arbitration agreement, declare that agreement to be void or even hear a claim to that effect? The answer is simple: the basis for the competence-competence principle lies not in the arbitration agreement, but in the arbitration laws of the country where the arbitration is held and, more generally, in the laws of all countries liable to recognize an award made by arbitrators concerning their own jurisdiction". See also Sandra Synková, *Courts' Inquiry into Arbitral Jurisdiction at the Pre-Award Stage: A Comparative Analysis of the English, German and Swiss Legal Order* (Vienna: Springer, 2013), Ch. 1, *passim* and especially at 65 (describing this aspect of *competence de la competence* as a "pragmatic fiction").

[17] Mahmud and McIntosh, *supra* n 15.

[18] The decision to register a request for arbitration is taken under Article 36(3) of the ICSID Convention, and ICSID Institution Rule 6(2) states that "[a] proceeding under the Convention shall be deemed to have been instituted on the date of the registration of the request". See Christoph Schreuer *et al.*, *The ICSID Convention: A Commentary*, 2nd ed. (Cambridge: CUP, 2009), at 469-473.

[19] See especially ICTY Appeals Chamber, *Tadić*, Decision on the Defence Motion for Interlocutory Appeal on Jurisdiction, IT-94-1, AR72, 2 October 1995, paras 14-22 (in favor of such a power, but, as pointed out by Judge Li, Separate Opinion, para. 2, confusing the question of legality with other jurisdictional questions) and the contrary decision, with discussion, in STL Appeals Chamber, *Ayyash*, Decision on the Defence Appeals against the Trial Chamber's "Decision on The Defence Challenges to the Jurisdiction and Legality of the Tribunal", STL-11-01/PT/AC/AR90.1, 24 October 2012, paras 36-54.

established on the grounds that the panel's terms of reference overlapped with those of a pre-existing panel on the same issue. The Panel responded to this as follows:

> The establishment of a panel is the task of the DSB. It is by no means clear that, once the DSB has established a panel [...] the panel so established has the authority to rule on the propriety of its own establishment. Nothing in our terms of reference expressly authorizes us to consider whether the DSB acted correctly in establishing this Panel.[20]

What, then, can be done about an invalidly established WTO panel? There are two options. First, the Appellate Body can decide on the validity of a DSB decision establishing a WTO panel. This would not be a question for the merits, but rather a preliminary question as to whether the conditions for the exercise of the Appellate Body's own jurisdiction under Article 17.6 have been established. This jurisdiction is dependent on the existence of valid panel legal determinations, which in turn depends upon such determinations having been made by a validly established panel.

Second, and perhaps somewhat more controversially, it is possible that the DSB is able to make legal determinations on decisions that it adopts under Article 6.1. This question has in fact arisen in a DSB meeting on Australia's request for a panel in *Australia – Tobacco Plain Packaging* in which Australia argued that the phrase "the DSB meeting following that at which the [panel] request first appears as an item on the DSB's agenda" in Article 6.1 meant the next meeting following that first meeting, not *any* meeting following that first meeting.[21] Many WTO members doubted that the DSB was competent to determine this issue, on the grounds that the DSB had no power to make any interpretation of Article 6.1. The primary concern was that if the DSB had the power to make such an interpretation, it would have to be by positive consensus, and this would permit a respondent to hold up the establishment of a panel. In contrast, the United States took the view that a decision to treat a non-consecutive meeting as a second meeting under Article 6.1 was necessarily an interpretation of that same provision.[22]

As a theoretical matter, the United States was correct. The DSB necessarily interprets the DSU every time it makes a decision, and this is because it is not possible to apply a rule to a fact (*in casu* by making a decision authorized by that rule) without at least implicitly interpreting

---

[20]   WTO Panel Report, *Australia – Leather*, WT/DS126/R, adopted 16 June 1999, para. 9.12. Despite this finding the Panel went on to make a determination on the issue. It found that the DSU did not require the disestablishment of a panel in the circumstances mentioned (at paras 9.13-14).

[21]   WTO Dispute Settlement Body, Minutes of Meeting held on 25 September 2013, WT/DSB/M/337, 13 January 2014, paras 4.1-4.67.

[22]   *Ibid.*, para. 4.44.

it.[23] But, it is submitted, this does not lead to the consequence feared by other WTO members. This is because the question whether there is an implicit or an explicit interpretation should be decided by the same procedure. Thus if an implicit interpretation is to be adopted by means of reverse consensus, the same should apply for an explicit interpretation. The result is that an explicit interpretation of Article 6.1 can be adopted by reverse consensus.[24] In principle, then, the DSB should not be precluded from determining whether its own decision under Article 6.1 is – or would be – valid. Indeed, one might say that it has a duty to do so.

2.3 Preconditions to the exercise of jurisdiction

2.3.1 Introduction

A validly established tribunal may still be unable to exercise jurisdiction if certain preconditions have not yet been satisfied. In many international judicial systems, an important precondition is an act of consent by the parties to the exercise of jurisdiction by the tribunal on a particular matter. No such precondition is necessary in the WTO, given that WTO members have *ipso facto* consented to the compulsory jurisdiction of panels and the Appellate Body.

There are however certain other conditions that need to be satisfied prior to the exercise of jurisdiction by a panel and the Appellate Body. Some are established by WTO law. Thus, a panel must be validly composed, and an appeal must be lodged by a valid Notice of Appeal. In addition, there is the possibility that there is a reason external to WTO law that precludes the exercise of jurisdiction by a panel or the Appellate Body, a condition commonly treated under the heading of "admissibility". Each of these conditions has arisen in WTO dispute settlement proceedings.

2.3.2 Internal preconditions

2.3.2.1 Composition of panels

According to Article 8.7, decisions to compose a panel are taken by agreement of the parties or else by decision of the WTO Director-General. In principle, there is no reason why a panel cannot review preconditions to the exercise of its jurisdiction, and indeed a panel has a duty to do so.[25] However, it is different in the case of composition, and this is because the

---

[23] Stanley Paulson, "Kelsen on Legal Interpretation" (1990) 10 Legal Studies 136.

[24] One might however then ask what is left of an authentic interpretation under Article IX: 3 of the WTO Agreement. The answer is that an authoritative interpretation is binding for future cases (and possibly past cases), not just the instant case.

[25] See above at n 9.

same logical paradox that affects a panel's ability to determine whether it is properly established, discussed above, affects its ability to determine whether it is properly composed.

This is confirmed by WTO jurisprudence. Three panels dealing with panel composition have denied that they can consider the validity of the decision to compose the panel.[26] In an appeal on the last of these, the Appellate Body agreed. It stated that:

> In our view, Article 8.7 confers on the Director-General the discretion to compose panels, which was properly exercised in this case. We therefore find that the Panel did not err in refraining [...] from making a finding on whether it was improperly composed.[27]

In fact, it is irrelevant whether the Director-General has a discretion to compose panels, but the result is nonetheless correct, for the reasons stated. On the other hand, the Appellate Body would be able to make such a determination, as it indeed did here. This is for the same reason as noted above in relation to the validity of the establishment of a panel, namely that might be necessary for the Appellate Body to determine in the context of determining whether it has jurisdiction itself.

2.3.2.2 Notices of appeal

Under Article 17.6 the Appellate Body's jurisdiction is "limited to issues of law covered in the panel report and legal interpretation developed by the panel". Under the Appellate Body's Rules of Procedure, these issues are to be set out in a Notice of Appeal which must contain "a brief statement of the nature of the appeal, including "a list of the legal provision(s) of the covered agreements that the panel is alleged to have erred in interpreting or applying".[28] However, the Appellate Body has refrained from treating the submission of a valid notice of appeal as a jurisdictional condition. Rather, the Appellate Body has preferred to see a valid notice of appeal in due process terms.[29]

For present purposes, it is to be noted that this has implications for the substance of the Appellate Body's jurisdiction in any given matter. If

---

[26] WTO Panel Report, *Guatemala – Cement II*, WT/DS156/R, adopted 17 November 2000, para. 8.11, WTO Panel Report, *US – Upland Cotton (Art 21.5 – Brazil)*, WT/DS267/RW, adopted 20 June 2008, para. 8.28, n 83; WTO Panel Report, *US – Zeroing (EC) (Art 21.5 – EC)*, WT/DS294/RW, adopted 11 June 2009, para. 8.17.

[27] WTO Appellate Body Report, *US – Zeroing (EC) (Art 21.5 – EC)*, WT/DS294/AB/RW, adopted 11 June 2009, para. 172.

[28] Rule 20(2) (d) of the Appellate Body Rules of Procedure. Cross-appeals are permitted.

[29] WTO Appellate Body Report, *EC – Bananas III (Art 21.5 – Ecuador II)*, WT/DS27/AB/RW2/ECU, adopted 26 November 2008, para. 280; WTO Appellate Body Report, *US – Offset Act (Byrd Amendment)*, WT/DS217/AB/R, adopted 27 January 2003, para. 206.

its jurisdiction is not formally limited to the claims made by one or more of the parties, other than to the extent that due process would be denied, then it follows that any Appellate Body determinations on legal issues in a panel report are limited solely by the scope of those legal issues that arise in a panel report and, separately, by the principle *non ultra petita*, according to which a tribunal may not make determinations that it has not been requested to make.[30]

2.3.3 External conditions (admissibility)

Whether a properly established (and composed) panel should exercise jurisdiction raises different issues. This question may be conceptualized in terms of the question whether there is an uncodified rule according to which that a panel should not exercise jurisdiction. Elsewhere in international law, this question is typically under the heading of "admissibility". As the ICJ has said:

> Objections to admissibility normally take the form of an assertion that, even if the Court has jurisdiction and the facts stated by the applicant State are assumed to be correct, nonetheless there are reasons why the Court should not proceed to an examination of the merits.[31]

There are many types of unwritten admissibility conditions, and these may also of course be codified. Some can also be subject to an express derogation, for example the rule on the exhaustion of local remedies.[32] A special type of admissibility condition concerns the conduct of a party to dispute settlement proceedings. In principle, a party may be estopped from exercise its rights to dispute settlement due to its conduct.[33] Can this type of condition be subject to a derogation?

This question arose in *Mexico – Soft Drinks*.[34] In this case the Appellate Body was asked by the respondent to rule that the Panel should have declined to exercise jurisdiction on the basis of the clean hands principle, according to which a party may be precluded from exercising its dispute settlement rights as a result of previous illegal conduct (the rule is a relative

---

[30] See below at n 42.

[31] *Oil Platforms (Iran v US)*, Judgment [2003] ICJ Rep 161, para. 29. For discussion, see Yuval Shany, *Questions of Jurisdiction and Admissibility before International Courts* (Cambridge: CUP, 2015) at 129-133.

[32] *ELSI (US v Italy)* [1989] ICJ Rep 1989, para. 50. The rule is dispensed with in the ICSID Convention.

[33] ITLOS, *Libertad (Argentina v Ghana)*, Order on Provisional Measures, Case No. 20, 15 December 2012, Joint Separate Opinion of Judges Wolfrum and Cot, paras 52-70.

[34] WTO Appellate Body Report, *Mexico – Soft Drinks*, WT/DS308/AB/R, adopted 24 March 2006.

of a simple estoppel).[35] The Appellate Body declined to accede to the respondent's request, on the grounds that to do this would diminish the dispute settlement rights of a WTO member under Articles 3.3 and 23, and therefore a decision to this effect would violate the panel's obligation not to "diminish" the rights of WTO members under Article 19.2.[36]

What, then, does it mean for a WTO organ to "add to" or to "diminish" valid WTO "rights and obligations"? It is suggested that this will occur when WTO rights and obligations are overridden – and therefore disapplied – by virtue of a non-WTO rule. This does not happen when a WTO norm is disapplied because of a contrary WTO rule (e.g. a WTO exception). This is because Article 19.2 does not prevent any *individual* WTO right or obligation from being disapplied. The use of the plural is significant; Article 19.2 protects *all* WTO rights and obligations seen as a package. And disapplying a valid WTO norm because of a contrary non-WTO right *does* diminish those rights and obligations, seen both singly and together.

The Appellate Body can be understood as saying that the DSU overrode the admissibility condition that was advanced by the respondent, while leaving open the possibility that there may still be a "legal impediment" to the exercise of jurisdiction in other cases. It has now emerged more clearly that such an impediment will exist when proceedings are brought contrary to good faith, in violation of Articles 3.7 and 3.10.[37] But does it go further than this? Could, for example, the exercise of jurisdiction by a WTO panel or the Appellate Body, as organs of the WTO,[38] violate or contribute to a violation of international law,[39] be considered such

---

[35] The clean hands principle was based on the *Chorzów Factory* case: WTO Appellate Body Report, *Mexico – Soft Drinks, ibid.*, para. 55 n 114.

[36] WTO Appellate Body Report, *Mexico – Soft Drinks, ibid.*, para. 53.

[37] WTO Appellate Body Report, *EC – Bananas III (Art 21.5 – Ecuador II)*, above at n 29, para. 228; WTO Appellate Body, *Peru – Agricultural Products*, WT/DS457/AB/R, adopted 31 July 2015, para. 5.25. See Bregt Natens and Sidonie Descheemaeker, "Say It Loud, Say It Clear: Article 3.10 DSU's Clear Statement Test as a Legal Impediment to Validly Established Jurisdiction" (2015) 49 JWT 873. As this author has argued in Lorand Bartels, "Applicable Law in WTO Dispute Settlement Proceedings" (2001) 35 JWT 499, at 501, this provision can, in practice, can be understood as "a conflicts rule limiting the uses of what could, *a priori*, be accepted as applicable law". On the other hand, contrary to what has sometimes been thought (e.g. Joost Pauwelyn, *Conflict of Norms in Public International Law* (Cambridge: CUP, 2003), 336), this is not an argument that Article 19.2 *is* a conflicts rule. It simply has the same effects. Pauwelyn, *ibid.*, at 478, also states that Article 19.2 is a rule of interpretation, which it is not.

[38] Articles 2(c) and 6(1) of the Articles on Responsibility of International Organizations (ARIO), annexed to UNGA Res 66/100, UN Doc A/Res/66/100, 27 February 2012.

[39] On the responsibility of the WTO, see Noemi Gal-Or, "Responsibility of the WTO for Breach of an International Obligation under the Draft Articles on Responsibility of International Organizations" (2012) 50 Canadian Yearbook of International Law 197 and Noemi Gal-Or and Cedric Ryngaert, "From Theory to Practice: Exploring the Relevance of the Draft Articles on the Responsibility of International

an "impediment" as well? This might occur, for example, if a panel or the Appellate Body, ignoring the indispensable third parties rule, made a legal determination that infringed the rights of states that had not consented to their jurisdiction. It now appears clear that, other than if a claim having this result is considered not to have been brought in good faith, this possibility is preluded.[40] In short, Article 19.2 governs the application of all non-WTO law, even in jurisdictional cases.

2.3.4 Applicable law in relation to jurisdictional questions

It follows from the foregoing analysis that panels and the Appellate Body are not competent to determine all internal issues relating to their exercise of jurisdiction, or else the Appellate Body has chosen not to consider what might be considered a precondition to the exercise of its jurisdiction not to be such a condition. However, the Appellate Body is able to determine the validity of the establishment and composition of a panel, and panels and the Appellate Body are certainly able to determine other issues relating to the exercise of their jurisdiction.

Where such questions arise, and panels and the Appellate Body are competent to answer them, there are several sources of law that these bodies can – and must – apply. Jurisdictional questions arise at the level of the DSU, which takes priority over any conflicting WTO rules, so it is not logically possible for a panel or the Appellate Body to resolve these questions by applying WTO rules other than those under which these bodies purportedly have jurisdiction (e.g. Articles 7, 11 and 17). However, this does not mean that these provisions are the only applicable provisions. In order to determine whether these provisions are valid and applicable, WTO panels and the Appellate Body would have to apply rules of international law governing these provisions. In fact, as discussed, Article 19.2 precludes them from applying such metanorms. On the other hand, in order to determine whether these provisions apply to the facts at issue (namely, a "matter" or valid "appeal"), it might be necessary to make legal determinations based on other legal systems. So, for example, ICSID investment tribunals apply domestic law to determine whether there has been an "investment" or whether a claimant has a relevant "nationality". It cannot be excluded that similar questions might arise in the WTO, for example, if it is alleged that a given respondent is not a WTO Member. To date, however, such questions have not arisen.

Organizations (DARIO) – The Responsibility of the WTO and the UN" (2010) 13 GLJ 511. It may be asked whether such a recommendation could amount to coercion within the meaning of Article 16 ARIO, *ibid.*

[40] See above at n 36.

2.4 Material scope of jurisdiction

Probably the most obvious jurisdictional questions are whether a claim is within the terms of reference of a panel, or within the scope of an appeal to the Appellate Body,[41] whether a panel (or conceivably the Appellate Body) has failed to determine an issue before it in violation of Article 7.2, which states that "[p]anels shall address the relevant provisions in any covered agreement/s cited by the parties to the dispute",[42] or whether a panel has discharged its duty under Article 11 (discussed below). From the perspective of applicable law, these questions are resolved relatively straightforwardly according to the relevant WTO provisions.

More complicated, from this perspective, are those jurisdictional questions that depend upon the application of rules that are not expressly set out in the DSU, such as whether a panel (or conceivably the Appellate Body) has made a determination on matters outside the scope of its jurisdiction in violation of the principle *non ultra petita*, or whether due process has been observed.[43] It may be thought that such questions involve the application of rules of "international procedural law".[44] However, the better view might be that such rules are internal to the WTO, and are devised and applied by panels and the Appellate Body in the exercise of their powers to conduct proceedings, especially taking into account the injunction in Article 3.3 that the WTO dispute settlement system "serves to preserve the rights and obligations of Members under the covered agreements".[45] On this view, the rules

---

[41] There have been numerous disputes on these issues. See, e.g., WTO, *Analytical Index*, 3rd ed. (Cambridge: CUP, 2011), updated at <www.wto.org/english/res_e/booksp_e/analytic_index_e/ai_new_dev_e.pdf (accessed 28 March 2016), on Articles 6, 7 and 17>.

[42] This provision, reflective of the principle *non infra petita*, requires panels to answer questions that are necessary to resolve the dispute, although questions can also be ignored on the grounds of judicial economy. See, e.g., WTO Appellate Body Report, *US – Upland Cotton*, WT/DS267/AB/R, adopted 21 March 2005, para. 732. Note however that Sir Hersch Lauterpacht was skeptical of the principle of judicial economy: *The Development of International Law* (1958), at 6-7; see also Chester Brown, "The Inherent Powers of International Courts and Tribunals" (2005) 76 British Yearbook of International Law 195, at 233.

[43] Panels are bound by the *non ultra petita* rule: WTO Appellate Body, *Chile – Price Band System (Article 21.5 – Argentina)*, WT/DS207/AB/RW, adopted 23 October 2002, para. 173. The same no doubt applies to the Appellate Body. On the admissibility of "new arguments", which is essentially a due process issue, see WTO Appellate Body, *US – COOL (Art 21.5 – Canada and Mexico)*, WT/DS384/AB/RW, 29 May 2015, para. 5.349.

[44] See also below at n 50.

[45] See also WTO Appellate Body Report, *US – Continued Suspension*, WT/DS320/AB/R, Annex IV (Procedural Ruling, 10 July 2008), para. 7, where the Appellate Body stated that "The conduct and organization of the oral hearing falls within the authority of the Appellate Body (*compétence de la compétence*) pursuant to Rule 27

of "international procedural law" are no more than an inspiration for endogenous WTO procedural rules.

3. Jurisdiction on the merits

3.1 Introduction

As a matter of legal theory, one can say that the primary function of a panel and the Appellate Body is to apply the relevant law, set out in the covered agreements, to the relevant facts, a process of simple subsumption. But to do so inevitably, even if implicitly, requires three prior determinations: the first is to identify the relevant facts (a function that is limited to panels); the second is to identify the relevant law; and the third is to determine the "applicability" of that relevant law to the relevant facts. The following discusses the way that these three prior determinations may be made, in light of Articles 7.1 and 11 and existing WTO jurisprudence.

3.2 The "matter"

The substantive jurisdiction of panels is set out in Article 11 and in specific panel terms of reference adopted in accordance with Article 7. Article 11 states that:

> [a] panel should make an objective assessment of the matter before it, including an objective assessment of the facts of the case and the applicability of [the relevant covered agreements to the facts of the case] and [the] conformity [of the facts of the case] with the relevant covered agreements.[46]

Standard terms of reference[47] are described in Article 7.1 as follows:

> To examine, in the light of the relevant provisions in (name of the covered agreement/s cited by the parties to the dispute), the matter referred to the

---

of the Working Procedures". It is not clear why this is described as *compétence de la compétence*, but the point is still valid.

[46] In order to make grammatical sense of this sentence it is necessary to add a definite article and certain genitive compound noun phrases, here set out in square brackets.

[47] Under Article 7.3 a complainant may also request the establishment of a panel with non-standard terms of reference. If the parties agree, a panel with non-standard terms of reference will be established. But Article 7.3 also states that "the DSB may authorize its Chairman to draw up the terms of reference of the panel in consultation with the parties to the dispute subject to the provisions of paragraph 7.1 above". This may mean that the Chairman may impose terms of reference on parties in the absence of agreement. See WTO Dispute Settlement Body, *Australia – Salmonids, Communication from the Chairman of the DSB*, WT/DS21/5, 23 July 1999, para. 3.

DSB by (name of party) in document DS/… and to make such findings as will assist the DSB in making the recommendations or in giving the rulings provided for in that/those agreement/s.

The Appellate Body has explained that the "matter", for the purposes of Article 7.1, comprises the legal claims and measures set out in that panel request.[48] A panel's terms of reference are therefore dependent on the panel request, which explains why any aspects of a panel request that are invalid are to be treated as severed from the resulting panel's terms of reference. As the Appellate Body has said, "Article 6.2 of the DSU lays out the key requirements for a panel request and, by implication, the establishment of a panel's terms of reference under Article 7.1 of the DSU".[49] However, there is another problem. If the "matter" already includes the "relevant provisions [of the covered agreements] cited by the complainant", then it makes no logical sense to apply these provisions to themselves. The problem could perhaps be avoided if the "matter" in Article 7.1 (as opposed to the "matter" in Article 11) were read as meaning simply the facts of the matter, as opposed to the law of the matter.

3.3 Identifying the facts

How to determine the facts of the matter is not straightforward. Article 13 and Appendix 4 give panels the power to seek information from sources they consider appropriate, and special provisions such as Annex V of the SCM Agreement establish certain procedures for providing evidence. The appropriate standard of review derives from Article 11,[50] and Panel Working Procedures can also set out certain matters relevant to evidentiary issues. However, beyond this there are no detailed WTO rules of evidence, *per se*. On what basis, then, can such rules be established? Georges Abi-Saab has proposed that rules "[one] has to go to the general principles of international procedural law which govern the exercise of

---

[48] WTO Appellate Body Report, *US – Products from China*, WT/DS449/AB/R, adopted 22 July 2014, para. 4.6. This is no doubt because, contrary to Article 7.1, what is submitted to the DSB is a panel request, not a "matter", *per se*. However, if the "matter" already includes the "relevant provisions" of the covered agreements cited, inter alia, by the complainant, it makes no sense to apply these provisions to themselves. The problem could perhaps be avoided if the "matter" in Article 7.1 (as opposed to the "matter" in Article 11) were read as meaning simply the facts of the matter, as opposed to the law of the matter.

[49] WTO Appellate Body Report, *EC – Fasteners (China)*, WT/DS397/AB/R, adopted 28 July 2011, para. 562. This presupposes that there is a valid panel request.

[50] This is made clearer in the Appellate Body's statements on the appropriate standard of review, e.g., in Appellate Body Report, *EC – Hormones*, WT/DS26/AB/R, adopted 13 February 1998, paras 116-119.

the judicial function".[51] However, in practice, the WTO Appellate Body has at most borrowed such rules from such general principles of law;[52] it has not, however, strictly speaking, applied such rules directly to the facts at issue. This can be justified on several grounds. One is, as with the burden of proof, to identify the formal source of such rules as Article 11. Another is to find the authority of panels to establish evidentiary rules in their inherent power to make determinations on the matters before them or, perhaps, as powers implied in the provisions establishing their duty to make such determinations.

3.4 Identifying the relevant law: the role of the parties to the dispute

Article 7.1 requires a panel to examine the "matter" "in the light of the relevant provisions [...] cited by the parties to the dispute". In contrast, Article 11 states that a panel is required to determine the "[the] conformity [of the facts of the case] with the relevant covered agreements", without any reference to the role of the "parties to the dispute". This raises an interesting question, which is the extent to which Article 11 authorizes, and perhaps even requires, a panel to apply "relevant" parts of the covered agreements even if this has not been cited by the "parties to the dispute" as required by Article 7.1.

Practice varies on this question. In *US – Gambling*, the Appellate Body said:

> In the context of affirmative defences [...] a responding party must invoke a defence and put forward evidence and arguments in support of its assertion that the challenged measure satisfies the requirements of the defence. When a responding party fulfils this obligation, a panel may rule on whether the challenged measure is justified under the relevant defence, relying on arguments advanced by the parties or developing its own reasoning. The same applies to rebuttals. A panel may not take upon itself to rebut the claim (or defence) where the responding party (or complaining party) itself has not done so.[53]

In other words, if, for whatever reason, a party does not mount or rebut a defense, a WTO panel may very well *know* the law,[54] but it not

---

[51] Georges Abi-Saab, "The WTO Dispute Settlement and General International Law" in Rufus Yerxa and Bruce Wilson (eds.), *Key Issues in WTO Dispute Settlement: The First Ten Years* (Cambridge: CUP, 2005), at 10.

[52] E.g. on the burden of proof, WTO Appellate Body Report, *US – Wool Shirts and Blouses*, WT/DS33/AB/R, adopted 23 May 1997, at p. 14.

[53] WTO Appellate Body Report, *US – Gambling*, WT/DS285/AB/R, adopted 20 April 2005, para. 282 (emphasis added).

[54] Cf. *Lotus*, above at n 2, p.°31.

only has no duty to apply the law,[55] but it is even unable to *apply* that law. Effectively, this means reading the phrase "relevant covered agreements" in Article 11 as a reference to the covered agreements, and their provisions, that are cited by the parties to the dispute.

On the other hand, a more expansive interpretation of Article 11 is evidenced by those disputes for which the panels' terms of reference do not include any mention of the respondent party to the dispute. Such terms of reference, where the phrase "parties to the dispute" in Article 7.1 is replaced by the name of the complainant(s), were standard in the first decade and a half of the WTO's existence. For example, the terms of reference of the panel in *US – Gasoline* were:

> To examine, in the light of the relevant provisions of the covered agreements cited by Venezuela in document WT/DS2/2 and by Brazil in document WT/DS4/2, the matters referred to the DSB by Venezuela and Brazil in those documents and to make such findings as will assist the DSB in making the recommendations or in giving the rulings provided for in those agreements.[56]

Since 2009, however, terms of reference retain the term "parties to the dispute", as follows:

> To examine, in the light of the relevant provisions in the covered agreements cited by the parties to the dispute, the matter referred to the DSB by the United States, Japan and the Separate Customs Territory of Taiwan, Penghu, Kinmen and Matsu in document WT/DS375/8, WT/DS376/8 and WT/DS377/6, and to make such findings as will assist the DSB in making the recommendations or in giving the rulings provided for in those agreements.[57]

According to the United States in *EC – Hormones* "[t]he objective [of this wording] was to make it possible for a defending party to 'cite' agreements additional to those cited by the complaining party, and to have the panel apply all agreements cited by both sides".[58] Textually, however, the phrase "relevant provisions in the covered agreements cited by the parties to the dispute" in Article 7.1 can also be read as referring to any provisions in the covered agreements that are cited by the parties

---

[55] For such a duty, see *Fisheries Jurisdiction (UK v Iceland)*, Judgment [1974] ICJ Rep 3, para. 17 and *Nicaragua (Nicaragua v USA)*, Merits [1986] ICJ Rep 14, at para. 29, although these were both cases falling under Article 53 ICJ Statute in which the respondent was absent.

[56] WTO Panel Report, *US – Gasoline*, WT/DS2/R, adopted 20 May 1996, para. 1.4. Emphasis added.

[57] WTO Dispute Settlement Body, *EC and its Member States – Certain IT Products – Constitution of the Panel Established at the Request of the United States, Japan, and the Separate Customs Territory of Taiwan, Penghu, Kinmen and Matsu – Note by the Secretariat*, WT/DS375/9, 26 January 2009.

[58] WTO Panel Report, *EC – Hormones (US)*, WT/DS26/R, adopted 13 February 1998, para. 4.268.

to the dispute, including exceptions cited by the respondent. Where the respondent is mentioned in the terms of reference, this explains why a panel might be limited to provisions that are cited by the parties, according to *US – Gambling*.

However, the question remains how a panel could consider such provisions if its terms of reference are limited to WTO law cited by the complainant. One answer might be that, under Article 11, a panel can apply an exception to the facts as a part of a "relevant covered agreement" even if that exception does not appear in the panel's terms of reference. This would mean that whereas the Article 7.1 limits the applicable law to provisions cited by the parties (even if only one), Article 11 allows, and perhaps requires, a panel to apply provisions of the covered agreements that it considers are "relevant". However, such a reading is not consistent with the Appellate Body's statement in *US – Gambling*.

3.5 The applicability of the cited relevant agreements

The next preliminary task for a panel or the Appellate Body seeking to apply the identified relevant provisions of the covered agreements to the established facts is to ensure that these agreements are "applicable". For a panel, this task is to be concluded in accordance with Article 11.

If one accepts that a rule is "applied" to a fact regardless of the likely outcome, as explained above, then a determination as to "the applicability of [the relevant covered agreements to the facts of the case]" concerns reasons external to that rule such that the rule cannot be applied to the facts at issue. In theory, there are several such reasons. One is that a rule is invalid (invalidity); another is that a rule cannot be applied because of a supervening norm (conflict); and a third is that a rule cannot be applied because of the conduct of one of the parties (good faith). In each case, the primary norm at issue is inapplicable as a result of the application to it of a meta-norm.

Aside from the considerations discussed above in relation to terms of reference under Article 7.1, it is uncontroversial that panels and the Appellate Body are able to make determinations that a WTO norm is not applicable to the facts at issue for a reason set out in WTO law, such an express exception.[59] For example, Article XX GATT states that "nothing in this agreement shall be construed to prevent [the adoption or enforcement of measures for certain legitimate reasons]". This provision,

---

[59] Jaap Hage, *Studies in Legal Logic* (Vienna: Springer, 2005) at 88, at 145-148. For uncodified rules an alternative (but problematic) reading is that the exception confines the rule. See Claire Finkelstein, "When the Rule Swallows the Exception" in Linda Ross Mayer (ed.), *Rules and Reasoning: Essays in Honour of Frederick Schauer* (Oxford: Hart, 1999). I am grateful to Federica Paddeu for this reference.

and specifically the phrase "nothing in this agreement", has the effect of rendering inapplicable any otherwise applicable rule, most obviously an obligation.[60]

More complicated is the question whether panels (and therefore the Appellate Body) are able to make such a determination based on non-WTO law, which in practice means the non-applicability rules discussed above. In principle, there should be no obstacle to making such a determination, subject to the condition, noted above, that in so doing panels and the Appellate Body do not add to or diminish WTO rights and obligations in contravention of Article 19.2. If one reads this injunction not to "diminish" WTO rights and obligations so as to ensure that these rights and obligations are not disapplied, which reflects WTO practice, this effectively removes the possibility of applying non-WTO law when it would have this effect. This is also borne out in practice, where WTO panels and the Appellate Body have refrained from applying non-WTO non-applicability norms.[61] Some contrary examples, such as the application of the non-applicability rule in Article 28 of the Vienna Convention on the Law of Treaties, can be explained on the basis that the Appellate Body thought (wrongly) that this was merely a rule of interpretation.[62]

This restriction on the application of non-WTO law with the effect of disapplying WTO law should not however be taken to mean that non-WTO law can never be applied in the exercise of a panel's (and Appellate Body's) jurisdiction. There is in fact a cardinal distinction between applying non-WTO law rules on the applicability of WTO law, which would diminish WTO rights and obligations, and applying non-WTO rules to anterior issues that require determination in order to determine whether there has been a violation of WTO law. Such legal operations fall within the category of the panel's (and Appellate Body's) choice of "legal reasoning", which the Appellate Body has made clear can be developed independently of any arguments made by the parties. In *EC – Hormones* it said:

> Panels are inhibited from addressing legal claims falling outside their terms of reference. However, nothing in the DSU limits the faculty of a panel freely to use arguments submitted by any of the parties – or to develop its own legal reasoning – to support its own findings and conclusions on the matter under its consideration. A panel might well be unable to carry out an

---

[60] See further, Lorand Bartels, "The Relationship between the WTO Agreement on Agriculture and the SCM Agreement: An Analysis of Hierarchy Rules in the WTO Legal System" (2016) 50 JWT 7, at 9.

[61] See Petros Mavroidis, "No Outsourcing of WTO Law? WTO Law as Practiced by WTO Courts" (2008) 102 AJIL 421.

[62] E.g. WTO Appellate Body Report, *EC – Sardines*, WT/DS231/AB/R, adopted 23 October 2002, para. 200.

objective assessment of the matter, as mandated by Article 11 of the DSU, if in its reasoning it had to restrict itself solely to arguments presented by the parties to the dispute.[63]

This reflects the ICJ's approach in *Arrest Warrant*, when the ICJ stated that the *non ultra petita* principle "[does] not mean [...] that the Court may not deal with certain aspects of that question in the reasoning of its Judgment, should it deem this necessary or desirable."[64] It is evident from this case (and others) that the central question concerns the ability of a tribunal to make legal determinations that are logically necessary for a determination on the question at issue.

It is in this context that one should understand the many determinations made by WTO panels and the Appellate Body concerning non-WTO law, such as the ruling of the panel in *Turkey – Textiles* to the effect that the EC-Turkey customs union had no legal personality,[65] the ruling of the Appellate Body in *Brazil – Retreaded Tyres* that "Article 50(d) of the Treaty of Montevideo [...] show[s], in our view, that the discrimination associated with the MERCOSUR exemption does not necessarily result from a conflict between provisions under MERCOSUR and the GATT 1994"[66] and the Appellate Body's determination in *EC – Bananas III* that various acts, such as "the allocation of tariff quota shares to ACP States exporting non-traditional ACP bananas" were required under the Lomé Convention.[67] One could even argue that such anterior determinations must be made as a result of the requirement in Article 7.2 discussed above.[68]

There is one striking exception to this practice, which the Appellate Body's statement in *Mexico – Soft Drinks* that it could not entertain an argument that would "entail a determination whether the United States has acted consistently or inconsistently with its NAFTA obligations" or would permit "panels and the Appellate Body to adjudicate non-WTO disputes".[69] This was because the "WTO dispute settlement system could [not] be used to determine rights and obligations outside the covered agreements".[70]

---

[63] WTO Appellate Body Report, *EC – Hormones*, above at n 49, para. 156.

[64] *Arrest Warrant (DRC v Belgium)* [2002] ICJ Rep 3, para. 43.

[65] WTO Panel Report, *Turkey – Textiles*, WT/DS34/R, adopted 19 November 1999, para. 9.40.

[66] WTO Appellate Body Report, *Brazil – Retreaded Tyres*, WT/DS332/AB/R, adopted 17 December 2007, para. 234.

[67] WTO Appellate Body Report, *EC – Bananas III*, WT/DS27/AB/R, above at n 12, paras 183 and 255(i).

[68] See above at n 41.

[69] WTO Appellate Body Report, *Mexico – Soft Drinks*, above at n 17, para. 56.

[70] *Ibid.*

How can this be explained? How can the determination of rights and obligations under the Lomé Convention be permissible but not the determination of rights and obligations under NAFTA? One explanation might be that the United States had not consented to a panel making a determination on NAFTA (even an incidental determination). By contrast, it could be argued that the EC had at least by implication consented to an equivalent determination insofar as it consented to the adoption of the Lomé Waiver, which rendered such a determination necessary. But the entire point of the *Arrest Warrant* and *EC – Hormones* dicta is that consent is not required for such determinations. Without more, it seems that the Appellate Body might have made a mistake in *Mexico – Soft Drinks* and, what is more, an unnecessary one, given that this was only a second reason for declining to consider Mexico's admissibility argument. But if the Appellate Body did make such a mistake, it is at least in the good company of Judge Higgins, who thought in *Oil Platforms* that the ICJ had "displace[d] the applicable law" by making a determination on the United States' right of self-defense when interpreting a national security clause. The problem in that case was not the anterior determination. It was that the determination was arguably unnecessary, and also that the determination was included in the operative provisions of the judgment, even though it was on a topic that was not included in the substantive jurisdiction of the Court.

4. Conclusion

This paper has looked at the law applicable in WTO dispute settlement proceedings at different stages of dispute settlement, and it has done so by focusing on the law that could be applicable and the competence of a panel (or the Appellate Body, and in some cases the Dispute Settlement Body) to apply this law to the matter at hand.

The first question concerned the legality of the establishment of a panel. It was suggested that current WTO jurisprudence is correct to deny panels the power to determine whether they are properly established, although this is not because the DSU gives them no express power to do so, but rather because as a matter of logic they are unable to come to an unbiased decision on the issue. This is by contrast no impediment to a decision of this kind by the Appellate Body, albeit this must be determined as a jurisdictional question as to whether there is a valid issue for the Appellate Body to determine.

The second question concerned preconditions to the exercise of jurisdiction by validly established panels and the Appellate Body. One such question concerns the composition of a panel, which a panel should not decide, but the Appellate Body can and should, and this for the same reasons as it cannot decide whether it is validly established. A second condition concerned the question whether a valid notice of appeal should be considered a jurisdictional condition; the answer is that it should not. A third question concerned the condition that a decision of a panel should not be exercised for some external reason (i.e. admissibility considerations). It was concluded that panels were precluded from considering this question because the result would be to diminish the right of a WTO member to dispute settlement, and this would be contrary to Article 19.2. This is the case even if the result would contribute to a violation of international law, thereby potentially engaging the responsibility of the WTO as an international organization.

A third question involved the law applicable to issues concerning the material scope of the jurisdiction of a panel or the Appellate Body. Insofar as these issues are determined by WTO law, they do not raise any complicated applicable law issues. The same cannot be said, however, for rules on which the DSU is silent. The view was adopted that such rules are issued in exercise of the powers of panels and the Appellate Body to conduct proceedings.

Finally, this chapter considered applicable law issues arising in relation to the merits of a dispute. This section began with an analysis of the "matter" before a panel, and then moved on to identify three separate judicial tasks that panels in relation to a "matter", which also apply, *mutatis mutandis*, to appeals before the Appellate Body. The first task is to establish the facts, based on WTO law established in the exercise of the inherent or implied jurisdiction of panels. The second is to identify the correct provisions of WTO law potentially applicable to those facts, taking into account the role of the parties in delimiting that law, and this task depends on an analysis of the covered agreements. The third task is to determine whether this law is applicable. This task could, in theory, require the application of non-WTO law, but Article 19.2 precludes any such enquiry. On the other hand, it was also established that panels and the Appellate Body should be able to make determinations on non-WTO law when this is necessary in order to reach a determination on a WTO issue properly before these bodies, provided that any such enquiry does not have the effect that WTO law is disapplied.

More generally speaking, it is possible to distinguish several different sources of law that are applicable in WTO dispute settlement proceedings. First are the WTO covered agreements themselves, which are applicable to questions relating to the material scope of jurisdiction of panels and the Appellate Body, as well as to the merits of disputes before these bodies. However, the covered agreements do not answer all possible questions. They do not, for example, determine when a validly established jurisdiction should be exercised, nor do they expressly say anything about procedural matters such as rules of evidence or due process. There might be a temptation to think that such rules, when they are devised and applied, originate outside the WTO legal system. The better view, however, is that they are inspired by such rules, but that they are wholly endogenous to the WTO system, and emanate from WTO panels and the Appellate Body in the exercise of their powers to conduct proceedings in accordance with the principles set out in the DSU. More complicated is the role of external rules that do not have a WTO analogue, such a rules on admissibility and on the applicability of WTO law. The ability of panels and the Appellate Body to apply such rules is essentially curtailed by Article 19.2, which prohibits panels and the Appellate Body from adding to or diminishing WTO Members' WTO rights and obligations. However, even Article 19.2 does not prevent panels and the Appellate Body from making determinations based on non-WTO law that are necessary for them to determine issues that are within their jurisdiction.

A Comment

Mary FOOTER[1]

I would first of all like to thank Jacques Bourgeois and the College of Europe for hosting us, and Jacques in particular for organizing this conference. It is both a privilege and a pleasure for me to be here today and to comment on Lorand Bartels' paper. My first two remarks concern applicable law in relation to some institutional aspects of the WTO and the Dispute Settlement Understanding (DSU).

Lorand mentioned the question as to whether the Dispute Settlement Body (DSB) is able to make legal determinations concerning decisions adopted under Article 6.1 DSU. Whereas some WTO Members think this is a problem while the US does not it just goes to show the kind of institutional schizophrenia that exists in the organization.[2] We talked in the first session about the disparity that exists between the judicial and the political branches of the WTO. There is a real institutional problem here that has not got better over time. Nearly twenty years after it was established the DSB (or at least some of its Members) does not feel capable of taking a decision concerning its power to interpret the DSU. Of course, the DSB, as a WTO organ, has the explicit power to interpret the Agreement for which it has responsibility.[3] Thus, I see no reason why this should not extend to interpreting Article 6.1 DSU.

The same goes for the issue of authentic interpretation. Claus and Lothar have written very knowledgably on this subject.[4] So far there has been no authentic interpretation under Article IX:2 of the WTO Agreement, unlike other international organizations where it does not seem to be a regular problem. However, I do not see this happening anytime soon in the WTO. It could be because the membership simply does not understand the power that it has or, if it does, it lacks the political will to exercise it, which is another matter altogether. Of course there

---

[1] Professor of International Economic Law, School of Law, University of Nottingham.

[2] Mary E Footer, *An Institutional and Normative Analysis of the World Trade Organization* (Leiden/Boston: Martinus Nijhoff Publishers, 2006), p. 41.

[3] *Ibid.*, pp. 29 and 35.

[4] Claus-Dieter Ehlermann and Lothar Ehring, "The Authoritative Interpretation Under Article IX:2 of the Agreement Establishing the World Trade Organization: Current Law, Practice and Possible Improvements" (2005) 8 *Journal of International Economic Law*, 803-824.

may be a lurking fear among Members that by exercising the power of authoritative interpretation they are tacitly acceding to a revision of the WTO Agreement. These issues notwithstanding, in practice Members have not been prevented from adopting decisions, e.g. on annual budgeting, that are all but an authoritative interpretation in name.[5]

Concerning some of the issues that Lorand raises related to state responsibility, I would agree with his proposition that a "legal impediment" might be "when the exercise of jurisdiction by a WTO panel or the Appellate Body, as organs of the WTO" could "violate or contribute to a violation of international law", e.g. by "ignoring the indispensable third party rule". The question is if this were to occur, what rules would apply to such an infringement? Potentially this could be dealt with by the draft ILC Articles on the Responsibility of International Organizations[6] or more likely, the ordinary rules on State Responsibility, developed by the ILC.[7] Conceivably, this latter point is covered by Article 3.7 DSU in conjunction with Article 3.10 DSU. WTO dispute settlement is a form of ultimate remedy, to be pursued after all other good faith attempts at peaceful settlement have been exhausted, and where Members should exercise restraint in seeking to link "distinct matters" in complaints and counter-complaints.

Where I disagree with Lorand is that with the potential "legal impediments issue" we are confronted with the fragmentation of international law and this raises some interesting questions that so far have not been fully explored. In my view, this has nothing to do with fragmentation but everything to do with the issue of conflicts in public international law, except here the issue is bound up with an institutionalized form of dispute settlement. In fact, we do not spend enough time thinking about conflicts rules in the WTO itself rather than necessarily in relation to other areas of public international law.[8] Lorand has quite rightly pointed out that Article 19.2 DSU may effectively operate as a *de facto* conflicts rule, where for instance it is applied as a "supervening norm", as appears to have been the case in *Mexico – Soft Drinks*,[9] concerning the "applicability"

---

5   Footer, above note 2, pp. 266-67.
6   Draft articles on the Responsibility of International Organizations, 2011, adopted by the International Law Commission at its sixty-third session, in 2011, and submitted to the General Assembly as a part of the Commission's report covering the work of that session (A/66/10, para. 87), YILC 2011, vol. II, Part Two.
7   Draft articles on Responsibility of States for Internationally Wrongful Acts, adopted by the International Law Commission at its fifty-third session, in 2001, and submitted to the General Assembly as a part of the Commission's report covering the work of that session (A/56/10), YILC, 2001, vol. II, Part Two.
8   Joost Pauwelyn, *Conflict of Norms in Public International Law: How WTO Law Relates to Other rules of International Law* (Cambridge: Cambridge University Press, 2003).
9   Appellate Body Report, *Mexico – Soft Drinks*, WT/DS380/AB/R, adopted 24 March 2006, para. 53.

of WTO law to the dispute between Mexico and the US. Many would consider that if Article 19.2 DSU is not specifically drafted as a conflicts rule in the treaty then it does not operate as such. However, state practice – or more specifically – the practice of an institutional organ, as in this case, determines otherwise.

Moving on to my last two points, the principle of *non ultra petita* (or *nec ultra petita*, as some of us Latinists might say), i.e. a finding made on a claim that was not raised by one of the parties. Firstly, the principle of *non ultra petita* is quite different to applicable law. Whereas the latter is a body of law that is "applicable" to the dispute, the principle of *non ultra petita* deals with arguments raised by the parties (or rather not raised by them) but does not encroach on the "applicable law" of the dispute.

Second, aside from *EC – Bananas*,[10] it will be recalled that *non ultra petita* was an issue in *Chile – Price Band System* where the Appellate Body took the Panel to task for making "a finding on a claim that was *not* made by Argentina", with respect to the second sentence of Article II:1(b) GATT 1994 because that provision had not been the subject of claim before the Panel.[11] In doing so, the Appellate Body ruled that the "Panel had assessed a provision that was not a part "of the matter before it" and had therefore "not made an objective assessment of the matter before it", as required by Article 11 DSU. Instead, the Panel had made a finding on a matter that was *not* "before it" and had "acted *ultra petita*".[12] [Emphasis in the original]

My final point is that Lorand discusses the issue of the "matter" in relation to Article 11 DSU and Article 7.1 DSU and I think quite rightly so. Yet, what about the word "panel", especially in terms of admissibility and jurisdiction, rather than "applicable law" *per se*? Mention is made of the "panel" in the sense of the ordinary panel in WTO dispute settlement proceedings but what about other types of panels, for example, compliance panels, under Article 21.5 DSU? For example, where it concerns an Article 21.5 compliance panel, the matter "involves in principle, not the original measure, but rather a new and different measure to the one raised before the original panel".[13]

---

[10] Appellate Body Report, *EC – Bananas III (Article 21.5 – Ecuador II)*, WT/DS/27/AB/R/W/, adopted 11 December 2008, para. 280.

[11] Appellate Body Report, *Chile – Price Band System*, WT/DS207/AB/R, adopted 23 October 2002, para. 173.

[12] *Ibid.*

[13] Appellate Body, *Canada – Aircraft (Article 21.5 – Brazil)*, WT/DS70/AB/RW, adopted 4 August 2000, para. 41.

Panel Discussion: Business and WTO Dispute Settlement

Chair: Reinhard QUICK
University of Saarland

Panel: Peter CHASE
US Chamber of Commerce

Darya GALPERINA
Pernod Ricard

Adrian van den HOVEN
European Generic Medicines Association

Geert ZONNEKEYN
Evonik Industries

Reinhard Quick (RQ): It is said that the dispute settlement system was the "crown jewel" of the WTO. This has not always been the case. When I worked at the GATT Secretariat during my junior lawyer's training in 1981 my adviser told me that the GATT did not need any lawyers but economists. We have come a long way since 1981. The business community was much involved in the Uruguay Round of international trade negotiations, in particular in the subjects of tariffs, GATS, TRIPS, TBT and SPS and may be to a minor extent in dispute settlement. This has changed as well. Today the WTO membership in the DDA negotiations only seems to concentrate on lowering of ambitions which, in turn, results in the business community's lack of appetite for yet another window of opportunity. In contrast to the rule-making function of the WTO business is very interested in a reliable and foreseeable system of interpretation. The Appellate Body has a remarkable record of clarifying some of the hotly debated issues such as the non-discrimination principle or the scope of Article XX GATT. Ten years ago when we debated "The WTO at Ten" there were discussions on transparency, *amicus curiae*, remand, creative interpretation or judicial economy. Some of these issues are still in discussion today but overall the system works.

I would like the panelists to address three issues. First, how do business people handle potential WTO cases? We should discuss the functioning of the Commission's Market Access Working Groups, which could be at the forefront of potential dispute settlement cases. Second, the importance of dispute settlement reports for our daily activities, and in particular the evolving interpretations of certain important GATT terms, e.g. "necessity" in Article XX (b) GATT. Third, implementation, or the lack of it: how do we cope with authorized retaliatory measures? And lastly dispute settlement multilaterally and/or bilaterally: what can we learn from WTO dispute settlement for the TTIP ISDS discussions?

Darya Galperina (DG): Pernod Ricard, the company that I represent, is a world export leader in wines and spirits; it operates globally from a European basis. The European wines and spirits sector at large has considerable export interests. WTO in general and WTO dispute settlement is important to us for several reasons: firstly because of the public sector's focus on regulation and taxation of our products. We recognize that balanced regulations and a proper level of taxation as a necessary means to protect the consumer, but often we are faced with inconsistent or discriminatory regulatory schemes. Furthermore our sector is very traditional with local or regional products often protected by GIs so that a shift of production for reasons of comparative advantage is not always possible. The multilateral rules based trading system is a guarantee for non-discriminatory market access. As you know tax and customs matters were at the forefront of several highly important WTO cases concerning my sector, e.g. Japan or Korea. These cases provided the members of the WTO with the necessary guidance on how to adopt tax and other product regulations in a non-discriminatory way. The interpretation of "likeness" and of "directly competitive and substitutable products" showed how the Appellate Body interpreted the non-discrimination principle contained in Article III GATT and helped my sector, inter alia, to increase its export performance. We benefitted from WTO cases and we highly value the possibility to discuss with the European Commission on whether or not to start a dispute settlement case. The decisions made in Geneva also help to address discriminatory practices in other countries in that they send a clear signal. Whether they prevent these countries from adopting non-GATT compliant tax – and other product regulations, however, is another question. In many instances countries do not have discriminatory tax systems by accident: such systems are often deliberate due to strong internal pressures. Strong external pressures, such as a WTO case, are often needed to overcome the strong domestic forces in the country concerned. In other words WTO rulings seem necessary for countries to act and change domestic practice.

It is all the more astonishing then that notwithstanding the strong GATT case law on non-discrimination we still have a number of discriminatory practices around the world. A good example is the tax situation in Thailand which illustrates how we approach the different avenues which are available to us. Ten years ago Thailand was an important market for our products. Then between 2005 and 2013 our exports declined considerably while at the same time sales of local products increased. We have been raising the issue of discriminatory taxation with Thailand since 2008 and the country did change its legislation, yet the discrimination continued. What is next? The next step is the Commission. We raise the issue with the Commission, provide information and discuss the situation. All this requires preparation: we have to convince the Commission that our arguments are valid so we screen them thoroughly on the basis of WTO case law. We then ask the Commission to use its diplomatic channels to have the discriminatory action stopped. If the diplomatic initiative is unsuccessful a decision must be taken on whether to take the case to the WTO. In taking this decision though the Commission will not necessarily be guided by WTO legal arguments, it will also look at the case from a political angle. This means that industry and the Commission might assess the necessity for action quite differently and at the end the Commission might decide not to bring a case. Of course the industry could officially request an initiative based on the European Union's Trade Barriers Regulation, but what would be the use of it if the Commission considers that, for political reasons, the case should not be brought to Geneva? This situation might explain why the above mentioned Regulation has been used so scarcely. Should an industrial sector even if it has strong legal arguments risk being exposed to a public decision of the Commission not to start a dispute settlement procedure in Geneva. Practically we have no other possibility but to exert pressure and to cite the existing WTO cases on non-discrimination in support of our position. We are wondering however whether the Commission applies a quota system on the amount of dispute settlement cases which will be brought yearly to the WTO. It seems to us that the Commission is quite reticent to initiate WTO dispute settlement even in strong cases. It is very selective not only with respect to the subject of the dispute but also with respect to the responding country. In such a situation the fact that industry cannot bring a case directly to Geneva is deplorable.

Another avenue would be bilateral negotiations in which the Commission could address and solve the issue if it happens to negotiate. We would prefer however that the Commission brought more cases to Geneva because this would intensify the discussions and help to stop WTO incompliant behavior. So, in conclusion I would suggest to the Commission to be braver and more aggressive and to use dispute settlement more as a tool to open markets, in particular since the market opening negotiations in Geneva are not delivering.

Peter Chase (PC): I appreciated Darya's remarks very much and would like to use them as a case study for my more general comments. The US Chamber of Commerce is a large business lobby in the United States; our main purpose is to promote a good business climate in the United States and abroad.

For business the rule of law is essential. Business needs to have a stable, predictable and fair system of rules precisely to prevent governments from arbitrary and capricious behavior as described by Darya. When it comes to our international activities the WTO provides for the stable environment. The US business community was a huge supporter of the GATT Uruguay Round and the WTO. The dispute settlement system enabled a leap forward in that it eliminated blockages and introduced a binding system for the settling of disputes guided by the "reversed" consensus rule. The WTO's dispute settlement system is a success. From a business point of view the rulings on non-discrimination and other GATT principles were important, so were some of the cases, e.g. gasoline, rare earth, auto parts, soft drinks or retreaded tires. The rulings shed light on the WTO's legal framework and can be used by business in discussions with governments about specific regulatory activities. Furthermore the compliance rate is remarkable. The WTO membership delivers.

One of the key issues we need to bear in mind is the very nature of the WTO. It is a treaty, a diplomatically negotiated agreement between countries. It is not self-enforcing. The membership does not see the Director General as a policeman who enforces WTO law. Cases are not necessarily brought for any violation but when there is enough pressure so that governments give up their diplomatic reluctance to go to court. The second aspect is its language. During my time in USTR I was part of the negotiating team in the Uruguay Round on trade related investment measures. Guess what, we were not very good at negotiating a precise legal text! Ambiguity is the nature of diplomatic negotiations. Another aspect is the rigidity of the multilateral system. You cannot just reopen the negotiations and change or improve the provisions. All these reasons call for an efficient and effective dispute settlement system.

My next point is our lack of standing to bring a case. We have to convince our governments, but governments have many reasons not to bring a case, as Darya said. So, in order to succeed we must build up the evidence present it to the government on a silver plate and beg them, only then will they consider acting. It is an uncomfortable situation having to rely on our governments espousing the case. I therefore think that we succeed only if the case has broad systemic implications. And quite often it means that you need more than one country to get it started. This is by the way an advantage for European business since it can assemble 28 specific national associations to support the case.

Next is the issue of precedent, an issue discussed to some extent in today's earlier panels. It would be useful to rely on precedents instead of having to re-litigate the issue. Another matter is the time-span of dispute settlement. In order to have an effective mechanism a timely ruling is of essence; and last but not least, compliance. You undertake all the efforts, the government accepts the case, your government wins and what happens then? If the issue is of administrative nature the government can easily comply with the ruling, yet it gets more difficult if a change in legislation is necessary. If the country does not deliver and retaliatory measures are authorized you find yourself in a delicate situation as a government official. In my time in government we had to look at withdrawal of concessions against Europe in the Bananas case. First we spent quite some time to figure out "how to hit best". We drew up our list and what happened then? Then we were told "camembert cheese and cashmere sweaters are important to our business". Clearly, retaliatory actions are not a solution: you "shoot yourself in the foot" in order to enforce compliance. So how should we address "compliance"? I am not sure I have many answers. Yet we as business community can exert pressure on our governments to comply with the rulings: if you lose, you comply! There happens to be a Pernod-Ricard case in the United States with which the US has not complied yet, the Havana Club. How credible are we if we do not comply with WTO rulings? Can we expect others to do so? Another enforcement avenue could be FTA negotiations. We could use bilateral negotiations as a way to enforce WTO rulings. In that sense the bilateral negotiations would strengthen the multilateral rule of law.

Adrian van den Hoven (AVDH): Today I would like to talk about the TRIPs Agreement and look more generally at enforcement as well as the impact of enforcement on the balance of competition versus exclusivity. The first issue that I want to discuss is the applicability of TRIPs in domestic law, an issue of considerable importance to the European generic medicine industry. As you know the European Court of Justice gave several different interpretations as to whether or not the TRIPS agreement could be directly applied. At first we thought this to be the case but had to learn thereafter that TRIPs was not directly applicable. The issue is highly political and hotly debated also with respect to other WTO Agreements. It touches on questions of whether the EU has exclusive competence. In my area, the generic medicines industry, the action was triggered by private enforcement. Take the example of which, before joining the European Patent Convention, had its own regime of IP protection, which gave the patent holder a shorter protection: 15 instead of 20 years. The interesting aspect of this case was that notwithstanding the fact that the patent was filed before the adoption of the WTO TRIPS Agreement, the Court nevertheless extended its duration for an additional 5 years. You will understand that the generics industry was not "thrilled" by this ruling, as they were excluded for another five years. The great challenge created by this and subsequent other cases is not only the issue of divergent interpretations and direct effect but more generally the negotiating capacity of the European Union in the area of intellectual property. The "ACTA debacle" is a telling example and probably shows the widespread resentment in some quarters against TRIPs.

The second issue I want to talk about is a WTO case which had been initiated but was settled, the famous transit case. Indian producers of generic medicines were exporting them to Brazil where the patents had expired. The medicines were shipped via Europe and were seized by customs officials in the Netherland on grounds of an alleged patent infringement in Europe initiated by a private party. This case again shows that a domestic enforcement action can easily lead to a WTO dispute.

My third point is the impact of TRIPs enforcement with respect to the balance between exclusivity and competition. I refer to the TRIPs case launched by the EU against Canada concerning the so-called Bolar exception and stockpiling. You will recall that the panel considered the regulatory exception (Bolar) as a reasonable exception authorized by TRIPS. This exception gives the generic company the possibility to produce the medicine for regulatory approval prior to the patent expiry so that it can be available on the market on the day the patent expires. In the same ruling the panel decided that the stockpiling of generic medicines – which actually served the same purpose, namely to be ready at the time of the expiry of the patent – was in breach of the WTO obligations. The decision had quite an impact on the moment from which competition should be granted in exclusive markets: the Bolar exception was favorable to generic manufacturers whereas the stockpiling was not.

This case brings me to my last point, namely intellectual property protection in free trade agreements. Here again, a balance between exclusiveness and competition has to be found. For example, how does the TRIPs MFN requirement affect the privileges normally only given to the FTA partner? It seems to me that Article 4 TRIPs is rather unconditional. The FTA practice of the European Union and the United States seems to strengthen exclusivity and enforcement without properly addressing the issue of abuse of IP protection. Although we have cases of abuse on both sides of the Atlantic I believe that the European Commission's and the United States' in current FTA negotiations are destabilizing the competitive balance contained TRIPs.

I hope that my short remarks show that WTO dispute settlement is not just an esoteric issue but has very direct consequences also on private party enforcement actions with respect to the TRIPs Agreement. In order to avoid another "ACTA debacle" the issue of balance has to be taken into account not only in enforcement but also in bilateral negotiations.

Geert Zonnekeyn (GZ): My presentation will be more general since Evonik does not have the same track record of WTO cases as Pernod Ricard or pharmaceutical companies. The lack of cases, however, should not be interpreted as if we are not interested in WTO law and WTO dispute settlement.

In preparing my speech, I was looking at the WTO website where I found a WTO business survey of February 2013. The WTO asked more than 300 businesses to tell their views on the WTO and its work. Around 95 per cent of the respondents were of the view that the work of the WTO was vital for businesses. The figure is not as high when it comes to compliance but still 72 per cent think that the WTO has been successful in ensuring that governments comply with their obligations under WTO law. The report thus seems to indicate that the WTO and the WTO dispute settlement system are crucial for businesses. But is this really so? In my company, for example, nobody is actually following developments under WTO law from nearby. That task is left to our trade associations such as Cefic or VCI. We do have a trade compliance department which focuses on trade issues such as export control and sanctions and the implications for the company. We are also intervening in anti-dumping cases if the product is of interest for our business, be it as a producer or as a user.

I do not want to repeat the statements made by my colleagues on how to convince the European Commission to initiate a WTO case. I would prefer to discuss the application of the EU Trade Barriers Regulation ("TBR") which was already briefly mentioned by Darya. As you know, the TBR gives companies the opportunity to submit a complaint with the European Commission against obstacles to trade maintained by third countries in breach of international trade rules, such as those laid down in the WTO Agreements. The TBR therefore provides for a participation of companies in the enforcement of WTO rules and is, as such, an indirect – albeit quite remote – route to the dispute settlement procedure of the WTO. When the TBR was launched in 1995, the Commission spent a considerable amount of time and resources in promoting the TBR in order to convince European industries to use this offensive trade policy instrument. This initiative was initially quite successful but the number of cases initiated by the Commission has decreased substantially over the last ten years. In total, 26 cases have been initiated but no new case has been opened since 2008 if I am not mistaken. The Commission seems to be less receptive to complaints than it initially was. What are the reasons for this decrease?

It is probably partially due to a stricter application of the substantive criteria for the assessment of complaints. It is remarkable, for example, that a TBR procedure was initiated by the Commission only after the complainant had threatened to submit an action for failure to act. In addition, in *United States – import restrictions on the import of prepared mustard,* an action for annulment was introduced by the complainant against the Commission's decision to terminate the procedure. Another, and perhaps more plausible explanation, is that EU industry prefers the "informal" route, i.e. direct recourse to the Member States and the Commission. In *Brazil-PROEX export financing programme,* for example, a TBR complaint was submitted only as a "second best" solution after the informal route did not produce any positive results. Similarly, in *Colombia – VAT legislation on imported cars,* France opposed actions under the informal route because a French producer was established in Colombia. It was only following the submission of a complaint under the TBR that an investigation was initiated by the Commission. These two cases seem to indicate that the TBR is used as a "last resort" when "diplomatic" action does not lead to any concrete results. Another and final reason might be that companies do not want to have their name quoted in the Official Journal stating that they are asking the Commission to attack, for example, China. The fear for retaliation is high.

I would tend to argue that the TBR has been made redundant by the Commission's Market Access Strategy (exemplified by the Market Access Data Base) and the Market Access Advisory Committee and Market Access Working groups. The Market Access Data Base contains important information on trade barriers in third countries. Regarding Russia, for example, you will find a quite impressive list of barriers. Ideally the data base should be empty. The Commission should perhaps be more vigorous and engage even more in diplomatic efforts or in negotiations with the third country concerned or in FTA or WTO dispute settlement to get the trade barriers removed. Having a data base *per se* is not sufficient.

Adrian has touched upon the issue of direct effect of the WTO TRIPS Agreement. I think we should reflect a bit further on the issue of direct effect of WTO law or international law in general. It is useful to have your dispute settled before the WTO in Geneva if the European courts in Luxembourg (the General Court and the Court of Justice) Luxembourg and most of the national courts refuse to give direct effect to WTO law. This implies, for example, that WTO Panel and Appellate Body reports are not enforceable before these courts. Moreover, in case of retaliation following non-compliance with a WTO ruling, companies that are subject to sanctions, are left empty handed. This was confirmed by the Court of Justice in the notorious *FIAMM* judgment where EU companies had asked to be compensated for the EU's non-compliance with the WTO ruling(s) in the bananas case and the retaliatory measures imposed by the United States further to non-compliance. There are two "exceptions" in the case law of the Court of Justice. Private parties may rely on WTO law in case a legislative act itself explicitly refers to WTO law (the *Fediol* exception) or in case the EU intends to implement a particular WTO obligation in a legislative act (the Nakajima exception). Recent case law (*Stichting Natuur en Milieu*) has demonstrated that the possibility left open by Nakajima will be further restricted and that companies will find it very difficult to enforce WTO law or international agreements before the European courts in Luxembourg. In addition, there is an increasing tendency in FTA's, to declare that the rules contained therein "*shall not be construed as conferring rights or imposing obligations which can be directly invoked before Union or Member States courts and tribunals*" (see EU Korea FTA).

As to Reinhard's last question how dispute settlement rulings influence our position in FTA negotiations I would like to cite the Chinese export restriction cases. They will have an influence on the energy chapter in TTIP since (some) US energy export restrictions (e.g. on liquefied natural gas) do not seem to be compatible with WTO law. I do hope that the Commission will use these arguments in order to negotiate a meaningful energy chapter in TTIP.

Financial Payments as a Remedy in WTO Dispute Settlement Proceedings

An Update

Marco Bronckers[1] & Freya Baetens[2]

Abstract

Remedies in international law present an intriguing challenge: what happens if a sovereign state refuses to comply with its obligations, even after an international adjudicatory body has ruled in its disfavor? The absence of compulsory enforcement arguably means that international law as a system lacks binding effect. The solution offered under the WTO system has been to authorize the prevailing Member in the settlement of a dispute to retaliate, if and when the respondent Member fails to implement a panel or Appellate Body ruling. Such retaliation can take the form of additional restrictions on imports of goods or services, or suspensions of intellectual property rights. Our paper examines whether fairer and more effective means of ensuring compliance could be inserted into the WTO system. First, existing remedy systems are outlined, comparing general public international law with the current WTO system, after which the EU compliance regime is analyzed. This is followed by an examination of the advantages of introducing the remedy of financial payments into WTO dispute settlement as well as a refutation of potential objections. The main elements of the subsequent proposal relate to the calculation, term, retro-activity and beneficiary of financial payments as a remedy. This version of our analysis updates a paper we published in May 2013.

---

[1] Leiden University; VVGB Advocaten/Avocats, Brussels (<marco.bronckers@vvgb-law.com>).
[2] Leiden University; VVGB Advocaten/Avocats, Brussels (<freya.baetens@vvgb-law.com>). We have benefited from the comments received during the conference "The WTO Dispute Settlement Mechanism: A Health Check" (Bruges, 12 September 2014), from Bernard Hoekman, Christian Tietje and other participants, from certain readers of the earlier published version such as Lothar Ehring and the research assistance of Hélène Marconi and Sophie Goelen. An earlier version of this paper was published in 16 *Journal of International Economic Law* (2013), 281-311

I. Introduction

Remedies in international law continue to present an intriguing challenge: what happens if a sovereign state refuses to comply with its obligations, even after an international adjudicatory body has ruled in its disfavor? The absence of watertight compulsory enforcement has led some to argue that international law as a system lacks binding effect.[3] The solution offered under the World Trade Organization [WTO] system has been to authorize the prevailing WTO Member in the settlement of a dispute to retaliate, if and when the respondent Member fails to implement a panel or Appellate Body ruling. Such retaliation can take the form of additional restrictions on imports of goods or services, or suspensions of intellectual property rights, from the offending Member.

In more recent times, it is increasingly recognized that retaliation has important drawbacks. For example, retaliation by countries with smaller markets has virtually no impact on offending countries. Furthermore, with retaliation, Members may easily shoot themselves in the foot by making imports from the offending Member more expensive. Retaliatory restrictions may also adversely affect "innocent bystanders", i.e., sectors (say, battery manufacturers) that have nothing to do with the original dispute (say, banana producers). Furthermore, retaliatory restrictions (on imports of batteries) also do nothing to alleviate the damages suffered by the sector (banana producers or traders) aggrieved by the WTO-illegal measure to begin with. Alternative remedies have therefore been proposed, and in this article we will take a new look at the introduction of financial payments.[4] These can bring pressure to bear on the offending Member to bring itself into compliance with its WTO obligations, and may also offer some measure of compensation to the parties damaged by the WTO violation.

Not all commentators, however, are critical of retaliation. Some are of the opinion that the current arrangements strike the right balance between what a multilateral system needs and what Members concerned about their sovereignty are prepared to accept.[5] Others have argued that

---

3   E.g., Hans J. Morgenthau, "Positivism, Functionalism, and International Law", 34 *American Journal of International Law* (1940), 260-84; Anthony D'Amato, "Is International Law Really 'Law'?", 79 *Northwestern University Law Review* (Dec.1984/Feb.1985), 1293-314.

4   This paper builds on Marco Bronckers & Naboth Van den Broek, "Financial Compensation in the WTO: Improving the Remedies of WTO Dispute Settlement", 8 *Journal of International Economic Law* (2005) 101-26.

5   This is a sentiment regularly expressed by trade officials: "if it ain't broke don't fix it", with some support in the literature. E.g., Alan O. Sykes, "Optimal Sanctions in the WTO: the Case for Decoupling (and the Uneasy Case for the *status quo*)", in Chad P. Bown & Joost Pauwelyn (eds.), *The Law, Economics and Politics of Retaliation in WTO Dispute Settlement* (Cambridge University Press 2010) 339-59.

any change will not bring notable advantages to developing countries; and that countries that violate WTO law cannot be expected to honor their obligation to pay damages either.[6] Yet others have gone so far as to suggest that, if anything, the WTO system should affirm more clearly that all WTO Members have the choice to comply with the rules, or deviate and compensate for damages if they believe that is more efficient.[7] In advancing our proposal for financial payments as an additional remedy in WTO dispute settlement to induce compliance, we will extensively engage with these contentions.

Our paper is structured as follows: first, we outline the existing remedy systems, comparing general public international law with the current WTO system, after which we make a brief excursion to the EU regime. This part is followed by an examination of the advantages of inserting the remedy of financial payments into WTO dispute settlement as well as a refutation of potential objections to this remedy. Subsequently we elaborate on the main elements of our proposal, before closing with a brief conclusion. As a preliminary clarification, the reader should note that our proposal of financial payments does not imply a plea to grant private entities access to the WTO dispute settlement system. The discussion below is predicated on the government-to-government nature of this system of dispute resolution.

Finally, a terminological remark: although it is tempting to speak of the remedy discussed here as financial "compensation", we have chosen the more neutral term financial "payments", so as not to prejudge that financial payments can also, if not primarily, serve the objective of inducing compliance.

II. International public versus private law remedies

Let us first recall how public international law handles wrongful acts, starting with the main aim (restitution), followed by its subsidiary solution (compensation), the available inducements to comply (countermeasures)

---

[6]   E.g., Jan Bohanes & Fernanda Garza, "Going Beyond Stereotypes: Participation of Developing Countries in WTO Dispute Settlement", 1 *Trade, Law and Development*, 4 (2012) 45-124, at 101-102.

[7]   See Alan O. Sykes, "The Remedy for Breach of Obligations Under the WTO Dispute Settlement Understanding: Damages or Specific Performance?", in Marco Bronckers & Reinhard Quick, (eds.), *New Directions in International Economic Law: Essays in Honor of John H. Jackson* (Kluwer Law International 2000) 346-57; Eric A. Posner & Alan O. Sykes, "Efficient Breach of International Law: Optimal Remedies, 'Legalized Noncompliance', and Related Issues" (7 March 2011) U. of Chicago Law & Economics, Olin Working Paper No. 546; Stanford Law and Economics Olin Working Paper No. 409, available at: <http://ssrn.com/abstract=1780463> or <http://dx.doi.org/10.2139/ssrn.1780463>, 20 (visited 22 June 2015).

and the mere declaration of non-compliance (satisfaction). Subsequently we situate the current WTO system of remedies in this context, before examining the EU regime experiences.

A. Remedies in public international law

1. Restitution

When a state infringes an international rule, this gives rise to a new obligation placed on the offending state to make "full reparation" so as to "wipe out all the consequences of the illegal act and reestablish the situation which would, in all probability, have existed if that act had not been committed".[8] Such full reparation takes "the form of restitution, compensation and satisfaction, either singly or in combination"[9] whereby preference is to be given to restitution, i.e., "to re-establish the situation which existed before the wrongful act was committed" insofar as this "is not materially impossible" and "does not involve a burden out of all proportion to the benefit deriving from restitution instead of compensation".[10]

In the *Genocide* case, the ICJ made reference to the decision of the Permanent Court in *Factory at Chorzów*, Article 31 of the International Law Commission [ILC] Articles on State Responsibility and its previous jurisprudence, to decide that:

> In the circumstances of this case, as the Applicant recognizes, it is inappropriate to ask the Court to find that the Respondent is under an obligation of *restitutio in integrum*. Insofar as restitution is not possible, as the Court stated in the case of the *Gabčíkovo-Nagymaros* Project, "[i]t is a well-established rule of international law that an injured State is entitled to obtain compensation from the State which has committed an internationally wrongful act for the damage caused by it".[11]

In short, only if restitution is not possible, compensation is to be paid in subsidiary order – which then covers "any financially assessable damage including loss of profits".[12]

---

[8]   PCIJ, *Factory at Chorzów (Germany v Poland) (Claim for Indemnity) (Merits)* PCIJ Series A No 17 [1928] 47.

[9]   UN ILC "Draft Articles on Responsibility of States for Internationally Wrongful Acts" (2001) GAOR 56th Session Supp. 10, 43 [hereafter ILC Articles on State Responsibility], Art. 34.

[10] ILC Articles on State Responsibility, Art. 35.

[11] ICJ, *Application of the Convention on the Prevention and Punishment of the Crime of Genocide (Bosnia and Herzegovina* v. *Serbia and Montenegro) (Judgment)* [2007] ICJ Rep 43, para. 460.

[12] ILC Articles on State Responsibility, Art. 36.

2. Compensation

Contrary to what is regarded in theory as the preferred remedy in international law, compensation is a commonly sought remedy in international practice but it has been awarded only rarely by the Permanent Court of Justice [PCIJ] or its successor, the International Court of Justice [ICJ]. In general, it has been suggested that "the Court is averse to awarding compensation",[13] although there are some exceptions. In its Advisory Opinion on the *Legal Consequences of the Construction of a Wall in the Occupied Palestinian Territory*, the ICJ, having referred to the dictum of the Permanent Court in *Factory at Chorzów* emphasized that, to the extent restitution was materially impossible, Israel was obliged to pay compensation:

> Israel is accordingly under an obligation to return the land, orchards, olive groves and other immovable property seized from any natural or legal person for purposes of construction of the wall in the Occupied Palestinian Territory. In the event that such restitution should prove to be materially impossible, Israel has an obligation to compensate the persons in question for the damage suffered. The Court considers that Israel also has an obligation to compensate, in accordance with the applicable rules of international law, all natural or legal persons having suffered any form of material damage as a result of the wall's construction.[14]

The ICJ is not always asked to determine the specific sum which is to be paid as damages – in which case it merely held that some compensation has to be paid while leaving the precise determination of the amount to the parties, as happened for example in the *Gabčíkovo-Nagymaros* dispute.[15] In *Cameroon v. Nigeria*, the Court was of the opinion that the injury allegedly suffered by Cameroon was sufficiently addressed by the "very fact of the present Judgment and of the evacuation of the Cameroonian territory occupied by Nigeria".[16] In the *Nicaragua* case and the *Armed Activities* case, the Court decided that it is only up to the Court to determine the form which reparation should take if there is no agreement by the parties.[17] On the other hand, the Court did order Albania to pay compensation to the UK in the *Corfu Channel* case.[18]

---

13   James Crawford, *State Responsibility, The General Part* (CUP 2013) p. 518.
14   ICJ, *Legal Consequences of the Construction of a Wall in the Occupied Palestinian Territory (Advisory Opinion)* [2004] ICJ Rep 136, para. 153.
15   ICJ, *Gabčíkovo-Nagymaros Project (Hungary/Slovakia) (Judgment)* [1997] ICJ Rep 81, para. 152.
16   ICJ, *Cameroon v. Nigeria (Judgment)* [2002] ICJ Rep 303, at p. 452.
17   ICJ, *Military and Paramilitary Activities in and against Nicaragua (Nicaragua v United States of America) (Merits)* [1986] ICJ Rep 14, para. 148; ICJ, *Armed Activities on the Territory of the Congo (DRC v. Uganda) (Judgment)* [2005] ICJ Rep 168, at p. 281.
18   ICJ, *Corfu Channel (UK v. Albania) (Judgment on compensation)* [1949] ICJ Rep p. 244 at p. 250.

Also, the Court established a compensation of $95,000 for the material and non-material injuries suffered by Mr. Diallo.[19]

Analysis of ICJ practice has shown a generally satisfactory compliance record for judgments and a more problematical one for provisional measures.[20] In this context, it would be relevant to note that the ICJ only clarified the binding nature of provisional measures relatively recently, in the *LaGrand* case.[21] For both types of decisions, the *Nicaragua* case marked "a paradigm shift as the last in a series of instances of open defiance and non-appearance", as noted by Schulte.[22] The authority of judgments or provisional measures has not subsequently been challenged in any significant manner. In sum, practice shows that countries found to have violated their international obligations and being ordered to pay financial reparation usually comply, albeit often with some negotiation as to the precise amount.[23]

In addition to the ICJ, several international tribunals have addressed issues of compensation, including the International Tribunal for the Law of the Sea [ITLOS], the Iran-US Claims Tribunal, regional human rights courts and investor-State arbitral tribunals. An overview of such case law can be found in the ILC Commentaries to the Articles on State Responsibility, including *M/V Saiga*, *Cosmos 954* and the decision of the UN Compensation Commission Governing Council concerning environmental damage stemming from the Iraqi invasion of Kuwait.[24]

---

[19]   ICJ, *Ahmadou Sadio Diallo (Republic of Guinea v. Democratic Republic of the Congo) (Compensation owed by the Democratic Republic of the Congo to the Republic of Guinea)* [2012] ICJ Rep 19, para. 56.

[20]   See generally Constanze Schulte, *Compliance with decisions of the International Court of Justice* (Oxford University Press 2004).

[21]   ICJ, *LaGrand (Germany / United States of America) (Judgment)* [2001] ICJ Rep. 502, para. 102 *et seq.*

[22]   ICJ, *Military and Paramilitary Activities in and against Nicaragua (Nicaragua v United States of America) (Merits)* [1986] ICJ Rep 14; Constanze Schulte, *Compliance with decisions of the International Court of Justice* (Oxford University Press 2004) p. 403.

[23]   David C. Baluarte & Christian M. De Vos, *From Judgment to Justice: Implementing International and Regional Human Rights Decisions* (Open Society Foundations 2010); Laurence R. Helfer & Anne-Marie Slaughter, "Toward a Theory of Effective Supranational Adjudication", in Beth Simmons (ed.), *International Law* (vol. 4) (SAGE London 2008) 95-156; Cecilia M. Baillet, "Measuring Compliance with the Inter-American Court of Human Rights: The Ongoing Challenge of Judicial Independence in Latin America", 31 *Nordic Journal of Human Rights* (2013) 477-495, at 488; Emanuela-Chiara Gillard, "Reparation for Violations of International Humanitarian Law", 85. *International Review of the Red Cross* (2003) 529-553, at 530; Francis E. McGovern, "Dispute System Design: The United Nations Compensation Commission", 14 *Harvard Negotiation Law Review* (2009) 171-193, at 172.

[24]   ICJ, *Corfu Channel (United Kingdom of Great Britain and Northern Ireland v Albania) (Assessment of the Amount of Compensation)* [1949] ICJ Rep 244; ITLOS, *M/V "SAIGA" (No 2) (Saint Vincent and the Grenadines v Guinea) (Merits)* (1 July 1999); Canada *Cosmos 954* Claim, 18 ILM 899 (1979); UN Compensation Commission Governing Council, Decision 7 (16 March 1992) Criteria for additional categories

International courts and tribunals have often assessed compensation for personal injury, historically mostly in the context of mixed claims commissions remedying State responsibility for injury to aliens.[25] This type of compensation is today mostly awarded by human rights bodies for material as well as non-material damage, the latter usually calculated based on an equitable assessment. In the last two centuries, many international claims have also dealt with compensation for damage to private property caused by internationally wrongful acts of States.[26] The reference point for valuation purposes is the loss suffered by the claimant as assessed "by reference to specific heads of damage relating to (i) compensation for capital value; (ii) compensation for loss of profits; and (iii) incidental expenses."[27]

3. Inducements to comply

International law does not contain extensive rules on measures to induce compliance with judicial decisions. Perhaps naively, the position seems to be that once a state has been held to have violated international law, voluntary execution is to be assumed.[28] One exception to this is Article 94(2) of the UN Charter which provides that:

---

of claims (S/AC.26/1991/7/Rev.1); see more extensively, ILC Commentaries to the Articles on State Responsibility, 100 ff.

[25] ILC Commentaries to the Articles on State Responsibility, Commentary to Art. 36, 102, paras. (17)-(18).

[26] Irmgard Marboe, *Calculation of compensation and damages in international investment law*, (Oxford University Press 2009); Borzu Sabahi, "The Calculation of Damages in International Investment Law", 553-95, in Philippe Kahn & Thomas W. Wälde (eds.), *Les aspects nouveaux du droit des investissements internationaux / Académie de Droit international de La Haye = New Aspects of International Investment Law /* Hague Academy of International Law (Nijhoff 2007).

[27] ILC Commentaries to the Articles on State Responsibility, Commentary to Art. 36, 102, para. (21); for further application and analysis, see Irmgard Marboe, "Compensation and Damages in International Law: the Limits of 'Fair Market Value'", 7 *Journal of World Investment and Trade* (2006) 723-59; R. Doak Bishop & Craig S. Miles, "Lost Profits and the Discounted Cash Flow Method of Calculation", 1 *World Arbitration & Mediation Review* (2007) 33-42; Charles Chatterjee, "The use of the discounted cash flow method in the assessment of compensation: comments on the recent World Bank Guidelines on the Treatment of Foreign Direct Investment", 10 *Journal of international arbitration* (1993) 19-27; Seyed K. Khalilian, "The place of discounted cash flow in international commercial arbitrations: awards by Iran-United States Claims Tribunal", 8 *Journal of international arbitration* (1991) 31-50.

[28] Elena Katselli Proukaki, *The problem of enforcement in international law: counter-measures, the non-injured state and the idea of international community* (Routledge 2010); Giuseppe Cataldi, "The Implementation of the ICJ's Decision in the Jurisdictional Immunities of the State case in the Italian Domestic Order: What Balance should be made between Fundamental Human Rights and International Obligations?", 2 *ESIL Reflections* (24 January 2013) 2.

If any party to a case fails to perform the obligations incumbent upon it under a judgment rendered by the Court, the other party may have recourse to the Security Council, which may, if it deems necessary, make recommendations or decide upon measures to be taken to give effect to the judgment.

However, this has never occurred as of yet.

There is one mechanism under general international law which is aimed at inducing compliance: the possibility for states to unilaterally adopt countermeasures. Countermeasures taken by an injured state (or, much more controversially, a third state acting in the common interest)[29] may solely affect "a State which is responsible for an internationally wrongful act in order to induce that State to comply with its obligations".[30] Such "[c]ountermeasures are limited to the non-performance for the time being of international obligations of the State taking the measures towards the responsible State" and they "shall, as far as possible, be taken in such a way as to permit the resumption of performance of the obligations in question".[31]

Countermeasures under international law have to comply with certain conditions in order to be considered lawful (and as such form a circumstance precluding wrongfulness of what would otherwise be an internationally wrongful act),[32] including prior notification and negotiation, although "the injured State may take such urgent countermeasures as are necessary to preserve its rights".[33] Evidently, some obligations under international law cannot form the object of countermeasures, for example the obligation to refrain from the threat or use of force or obligations for the protection of fundamental human rights.[34]

---

[29] Christian Hillgruber, "The Right of Third States to take Countermeasures", in Christian Tomuschat & Jean-Marc Thouvenin (eds.), *The Fundamental Rules of the International Legal Order: Jus cogens and Obligations Erga omnes* (Nijhoff 2006) 265-93; Martin Dawidowicz, "Public Law Enforcement Without Public Law Safeguards?: an Analysis of State Practice on Third Party Countermeasures and Their Relationship to the UN Security Council", 77 *British Year Book of International Law* (2006) 333-418.

[30] ILC Articles on State Responsibility, Art. 49(1); Naoki Iwatsuki, "Legal Structure of International Dispute Settlement and Countermeasures: a Reflection on the Legal Basis of Countermeasures in Contemporary International Law", 107 *Journal of international law and diplomacy* (2008) 72-105; Denis Alland, "The Definition of Countermeasures", in James Crawford, Alain Pellet & Simon Olleson (eds.), *The Law of International Responsibility* (Oxford University Press 2010) 1127-36.

[31] ILC Articles on State Responsibility, Art. 49(2)-(3).

[32] Hubert Lesaffre, "Circumstances precluding Wrongfulness in the ILC Articles on State Responsibility: Countermeasures", in James Crawford, Alain Pellet & Simon Olleson (eds.), *The Law of International Responsibility* (Oxford University Press 2010) 469-73.

[33] ILC Articles on State Responsibility, Art. 52(1)-(2).

[34] ILC Articles on State Responsibility, Art. 50.

Importantly, a proportionality requirement is built into the system as well: "[c]ountermeasures must be commensurate with the injury suffered, taking into account the gravity of the internationally wrongful act and the rights in question".[35] Furthermore, they "may not be taken, and if already taken must be suspended without undue delay if: (a) the internationally wrongful act has ceased; and (b) the dispute is pending before a court or tribunal which has the authority to make decisions binding on the parties".[36] Finally, countermeasures have to be terminated as soon as the responsible State is again in compliance with its obligations in relation to the internationally wrongful act.[37] These conditions again indicate that the sole purpose of allowing for countermeasures under international law is not for the injured state to obtain reparation of its injuries but to induce compliance with international obligations.[38]

4. Satisfaction

Finally, applicants before the ICJ may ask the Court to deliver a declaration of non-compliance, which does not entail any specific compensation, but merely the explicit pronouncement by the Court that the respondent has acted in breach of international law. The corollary hereof under the rules on reparation for injuries from internationally wrongful conduct is the duty of the respondent to provide "satisfaction". Such obligation arises from injuries which cannot be made good by restitution or compensation and "may consist in an acknowledgement of the breach, an expression of regret, a formal apology or another appropriate modality", while not being disproportionate or humiliating to the responsible state.[39] In its *Arrest Warrant* judgment for example, the ICJ concluded that its finding that the Belgian actions had infringed the international rules on immunity from criminal jurisdiction of Mr. Yerodia

---

[35] ILC Articles on State Responsibility, Art. 51; as previously already expressed in case law, e.g., *Air Service Agreement of 27 March 1946 (United States of America v France)* (1978) 18 RIAA 417: "[I]t is generally agreed that all counter-measures must, in the first instance, have some degree of equivalence with the alleged breach; this is a well-known rule. In the course of the present proceedings, both Parties have recognized that the rule applies to this case, and they both have invoked it. It has been observed, generally, that judging the 'proportionality' of countermeasures is not an easy task and can at best be accomplished by approximation" (para. 83); Thomas M. Franck, "On Proportionality of Countermeasures in International Law", 102 *American Journal of International Law* (2008) 715-67.

[36] ILC Articles on State Responsibility, Art. 52(3).

[37] ILC Articles on State Responsibility, Art. 53; Maurice Kamto, "The Time Factor in the Application of Countermeasures", in James Crawford, Alain Pellet & Simon Olleson (eds.), *The Law of International Responsibility* (Oxford University Press 2010) 1169-76.

[38] Math Noortmann, *Countermeasures in international law: five salient cases* (Gadjah Mada University Press 2005).

[39] ILC Articles on State Responsibility, Art. 37.

constituted a form of satisfaction which in and of itself made good the moral injury complained of by the DRC.[40]

A similar reasoning was followed in the *Land and Maritime Boundary between Cameroon and Nigeria* decision when the ICJ refused to order any further remedies.[41] In *Application of the Convention on the Prevention and Punishment of the Crime of Genocide*, satisfaction was awarded because restitution was not possible and financial compensation was not considered appropriate due to the lack of a "sufficiently direct and causal link" between the failure to take adequate measures to prevent genocide and the massacre at Srebrenica.[42] The approach of the ICJ towards satisfaction has been adopted and referred to by other courts and tribunals, for example in the *Guyana/Suriname*[43] and the *CMS v. Argentina* arbitrations.[44]

B. The present remedies of WTO dispute settlement

When WTO law is found to have been breached, the WTO Dispute Settlement Understanding [DSU] does not prescribe full restitution. It is generally assumed that rulings of WTO tribunals are only prospective in nature: the offending Member should bring itself into compliance by abandoning the contested measure and need not worry about the past.[45]

---

[40] *Arrest Warrant of 11 April 2000 (Democratic Republic of the Congo v Belgium)* [2002] ICJ Rep 31, para. 75.

[41] *Land and Maritime Boundary between Cameroon and Nigeria (Cameroon v Nigeria; Equitorial Guinea intervening)* [2002] ICJ Rep 452, para. 319.

[42] ICJ, *Application of the Convention on the Prevention and Punishment of the Crime of Genocide*, above n 9, para. 463.

[43] PCA, *Guyana/Suriname* (Award) (17 September 2007), paras. 451-2 and para. 485, quoting the ITLOS judgment in *The M/V "Saiga" (No. 2)*, above n 22, para. 171.

[44] ICSID Case No. ARB/01/8, *CMS Gas Transmission Company v Argentine Republic* (Award) (12 May 2005), para. 399; ICSID Case No. ARB/98/2, *Victor Pey Casado and President Allende Foundation v Chile*, (Award) (8 May 2008), para. 704; ICSID Case No. ARB/06/18, *Joseph Charles Lemire v Ukraine* (Award) (28 March 2011), para. 344; for a more extensive analysis of the latter two cases, see Patrick Dumberry, "Satisfaction as a Form of Reparation for Moral Damages Suffered by Investors and Respondent States in Investor-State Arbitration Disputes", 3 *Journal of International Dispute Settlement* 1 (2012) 205-42.

[45] Geraldo Vidigal, "Re-Assessing WTO Remedies: The Prospective and the Retrospective", 16 *Journal of International Economic Law* (2013) 505-534; Joost Pauwelyn, "The Calculation and Design of Trade Retaliation in Context: what is the Goal of Suspending WTO Obligations?", with comments by John Jackson and Alan O. Sykes, in Chad P. Bown & Joost Pauwelyn (eds.), *The Law, Economics and Politics of Retaliation in WTO Dispute Settlement* (Cambridge University Press 2010) 34-72, at 57. Note that the prospective nature of WTO rulings does not necessarily follow from the DSU such as Article 21 (3). That particular provision, giving offending WTO Members a "reasonable period of time" to bring themselves into compliance, could be read as extending a grace period during which the offending Member does not have to fear retaliatory measures.

This means that no attempt is made to fully redress the illegal situation, and to bring the offending WTO Member in the same situation as if the illegal measure had not existed. The DSU also makes no provision for reparation of damages caused by the WTO-illegal measure; nor is there any provision in the DSU for a declaration of non-compliance.

One of two things might happen in case the offending Member does not bring itself into compliance within "a reasonable period of time". It could offer compensatory trade concessions to the aggrieved Member.[46] This option has proven to be theoretical, as no domestic industry in the offending country is prepared to expose itself to more competition to "pay" for the maintenance of a WTO-illegal measure that is seen to benefit another, unrelated sector. Only very few cases of "trade compensation" have been reported in WTO history, when Japan offered additional tariff concessions on some imported liquors before bringing itself into compliance with the *Japanese Alcoholic Beverages* ruling,[47] or when Turkey offered concessions on chemical products, after having been found to restrict imports of Indian textiles illegally in *Turkey Textiles*.[48]

Alternatively, the aggrieved country is allowed to retaliate.[49] In public international law terms, trade retaliation can be seen as a countermeasure, exercising pressure on the offending member to bring itself in compliance. These countermeasures are held in check, by the stipulation in the DSU that the retaliatory measure can only suspend a level of concessions that is "equivalent" to the violation of WTO law (nullification or impairment) found.[50] Thus, the WTO Dispute Settlement Understanding has made explicit the proportionality requirement of public international law.[51]

There has been considerable debate amongst scholars on the objectives to be ascribed to this remedy of retaliation. As originally conceived, when the GATT was primarily a tariff-reducing mechanism, retaliation may have been thought to re-establish a balance of concessions. This could not really be characterized as "compliance" nor as "compensation" in a public international law sense. If a country following a finding that it has failed

---

[46] DSU Art. 22(2).

[47] WTO Appellate Body Report, *Japan – Taxes on Alcoholic Beverages, Report of the Appellate Body*, WT/DS8/AB/R, WT/DS10/AB/R, WT/DS11/AB/R, adopted 4 October 1996; Andrew W. Shoyer, Eric M. Solovy & Alexander W. Koff, "Implementation and Enforcement of Dispute Settlement Decisions", in Patrick F.J. Macrory, Arthur E. Appleton, Michael G. Plummer (eds.), *The World Trade Organization: Legal, Economic and Political analysis* (Springer 2004) 1341-69, at 1365-67.

[48] WTO Appellate Body Report, *Turkey – Restrictions on Imports of Textile and Clothing Products, Report of the Appellate Body*, WT/DS34/AB/R, adopted 22 October 1999; Simon Lester, Bryan Mercurio & Anwel Davies, *World Trade Law: Text, Materials and Commentary* (2nd ed., Hart 2012) 161.

[49] DSU Art 3 and 22(2).

[50] DSU Art. 22(4).

[51] See above n 35.

to implement certain concessions would be allowed merely to offer other concessions, so as to rebalance its overall basket or schedule of concessions, it cannot be said to "comply" with its original concessions. Neither the aggrieved Member, nor its affected private sector damaged by the disputed measure, normally obtains any benefit from retaliation, i.e., the rebalancing of concessions. Admittedly, some domestic industries in the aggrieved country, which are not in any way involved with the underlying dispute, likely obtain some additional protection from retaliatory restrictions – but this in a way is a "windfall profit" for them, which the aggrieved Member did not intend to obtain to begin with, and which from an overall economic welfare perspective is probably counterproductive as most protectionist measures are. It is difficult to characterize any of this as "compensation" in a public international law sense.

Over time, the inducement on the offending Member to comply came to be seen as a more important objective of retaliation.[52] The emphasis in the GATT/WTO system shifted from tariff concessions to rules (commercial and economic policy principles), in keeping with the traditional focus of public international law. Furthermore, to the extent that retaliation permitted the shifting around of any concessions or legal obligations, it was recognized that this would only be temporary, for as long as the offending member had not brought itself into compliance with its original obligation.[53] Indeed, although the text of the WTO Dispute Settlement is not entirely without ambiguity, we believe there can be little doubt that compliance is the preferred outcome of WTO dispute settlement.[54] This corresponds with past and present intentions of the WTO membership.[55] It is a central element of the WTO dispute

---

[52]   Jackson commenting on Pauwelyn, above n 43, at 66 – in his comment, Jackson distinguished up to twelve goals ascribed to international dispute settlement.

[53]   See notably DSU Art. 22(1).

[54]   We follow John Jackson's analysis ("The WTO Dispute Settlement Understanding – Misunderstanding the Nature of Legal Obligation", 91 *American Journal of International Law* (1997) 60-64; "International Law Status of WTO Dispute Settlement Reports: Obligation to Comply or Option to 'Buy Out'?", 98 *American Journal of International Law* (2004) 109-25) against Judith Hippler Bello ("The WTO dispute settlement understanding: less is more", 90 *American Journal of International Law* (1996) 416-18) and Sykes (above n 5).

[55]   E.g., Bohanes & Garza: "[E]very WTO complainant hopes for prompt and complete compliance", <http://worldtradelaw.typepad.com/ielpblog/page/2/> (discussion of their article "Going Beyond Stereotypes: Participation of Developing Countries in WTO Dispute Settlement", above n 4). For a typical sentiment of a Member see, e.g., EU Trade Commissioner Karel de Gucht, who stated in a speech to the Bavarian Industry Association on 21 September 2011: "Of course open trade can only work when its rules and disciplines are rigorously enforced. A good example is the verdict by the WTO which, last July, ruled against China's use of export restrictions of certain raw materials, backing a case jointly brought by the US, Mexico and the European Union. These materials are crucial inputs for the German manufacturing sector – whether producers of electronics, automotives, refrigerators or medical

settlement system to provide *"security and predictability"* to the multilateral trading system.[56]

Given this tenet of the WTO Dispute Settlement System, we also do not subscribe to propositions allowing Members to deviate from WTO obligations and remain non-compliant against payment of compensation, if they would consider such a breach of WTO law more "efficient".[57] Should this view be accepted, the WTO would regress from rule-based to power-based diplomacy, with an attendant loss in predictability and in equality amongst stakeholders.[58]

Having established then that compliance is the primary objective of WTO dispute settlement, we now turn to the question how this system could be reformed more in line with public international law combining pressures to comply with some grant of compensation to injured parties. Experiences with remedies in EU law provide food for thought.

C. Remedies in EU law

The EU likes to think of itself as constituting a distinct legal order of international law.[59] Still, the EU is an international organization and the relations between its Member States are treaty-based. The way the EU deals with treaty infringements is therefore also of interest to the present discussion.

From the early days, private individuals played a very important role in detecting Treaty infringements by Member States. They could alert the European Commission and ask the Commission to start a Treaty infringement action before the European Court of Justice. Alternatively,

---

equipment. The WTO found China's restricted export regime in breach of its international commitments and unjustified, regardless of the environmental concerns cited, because these are not and cannot be addressed simply by discriminating against foreign competitors. As a result, we also expect China to revisit its overall export restriction regime, and we will be closely watching the situation for the remaining restrictions on other raw materials". <http://trade.ec.europa.eu/doclib/docs/2011/september/tradoc_148205.pdf> (visited 22 June 2015).

[56] DSU Art. 3(2).

[57] Sykes, and Posner & Sykes, above n 5; see also Chi Carmody, unpublished work cited in Arwel Davies, "Reviewing dispute settlement at the World Trade Organization", 5 *World Trade Review* (2006) 31-67, at 59 (fn 91).

[58] We have taken issue with the "efficient breach" theory in more detail in our predecessor article, Bronckers & Baetens, above in the byline, at 291-295.

[59] See notably CJEU, Case 26/62 *Van Gend & Loos v. the Netherlands* (1963) ECR 1; CJEU, Case 6/64 *Costa v Enel* (1964) ECR 1194. For a vivid account of how the choices made by the European Court of Justice for EU law differed from traditional international law, see Morten Rasmussen, "From *Costa Enel* to the Treaties of Rome: A Brief History of a Legal Revolution", in Miguel Poiares Maduro & Loïc Azoulai (eds.), *The Past and Future of EU Law: The Classics of EU Law Revisited on the 50th Anniversary of the Rome Treaty* (Hart 2010) 69-85.

individuals could try and have a national court invalidate a Treaty-infringing measure of their national governments, by appealing to those EU law principles that are considered "directly effective" in the national legal order. National courts are able, and sometimes are obliged, to request the European Court of Justice, for interpretative guidance in so-called preliminary rulings. These were and continue to be distinct features of the EU legal order. Of course, one Member State can also sue another Member State before the European Court on the grounds that the latter is infringing EU law. This is more akin to the traditional position of government-to-government litigation in public international law.

Yet no matter how the EU Treaty infringement was pursued, to the extent a Member State refused to implement a European or national court ruling, thereby maintaining a Treaty-infringing measure, EU law made no provision for additional remedies. In fact, compared to public international law it was notable that an aggrieved Member State could not take countermeasures against the Treaty-infringing State that refused to bring itself into compliance with EU law. Nor did EU law envisage that Member States could request compensation from each other in response to Treaty infringements. Compared to the WTO's predecessor, the GATT, EU law differed too in that it did not incorporate a mechanism, such as the introduction of retaliatory trade restrictions, to induce recalcitrant Member States to comply with court rulings.

It was considered an important step forward in the EU system of remedies, when in 1993 the European Court of Justice obtained the power to impose lump sums or financial penalties on offending Member States that refuse to implement a prior Court ruling.[60] The EU Court has used this power 21 times from 2000 through the end of 2014. Lump sums, relating to the impact of the infringement on public and private interests and also operating as a disincentive to foot-dragging by the offending Member State, have varied from €1 to 40 million. Penalty payments are designed as a more direct inducement to comply, and have ranged from €16.000 to €316,500 per day. Lump sums and penalty payments can be imposed cumulatively.[61] The amounts depend on factors such

---

[60]   Now codified in Art. 260 TFEU (Lisbon Treaty). Note that in the particular case of a Member State failing to notify measures implementing a certain type of EU legislation ("directives adopted under a legislative procedure"), the Commission may ask the Court to impose immediately a lump sum or a penalty payment together with the establishment of an EU law infringement. See Art. 260 (3) TFEU. For what could have been the first application of the latter provision see CJEU, C-320/13, *Commission v. Poland*, Opinion of Advocate-General Wathelet of 11 December 2014; Order of the Court of 30 March 2015 (case withdrawn).

[61]   E.g., CJEU, Case C-196/13, *Commission v. Italy*. judgment of 2 December 2014. See generally Brian Jack, "Enforcing Member State Compliance with EU Environmental Law: A Critical Evaluation of the Use of Financial Penalties", 23 *Journal of Environmental Law* (2011) 73-95.

as the nature or seriousness of the infringement, its duration, and the need to deter future infringements, but also the gross domestic product [GDP] (ability to pay) of the country involved.[62] The amounts paid by the recalcitrant Member State are allocated to the EU's budget. Private stakeholders who may have been damaged by the treaty infringement obtain no part of these payments. Yet EU law obliges Member States to pay compensation separately to private parties who can demonstrate, in an action before their national courts, that they suffered damages caused by the national measure that infringed EU law.[63] Importantly, under EU law a Member State does not have the choice to pay financial penalties and/or compensation and continue with the infringement: the obligation to comply with EU law is paramount.

With this system of remedies the EU is similar to the WTO, in that it has created specific inducements for Member States to comply with court or dispute settlement rulings. While the EU's preferred instrument (financial sanctions) is different than the WTO's (retaliation) at present, like the WTO ("equivalence") it is also a requirement of EU law that the compliance inducement be proportional to the treaty infringement, and also to the Member State's ability to pay.[64] In other words, given the similarity in outlook between the EU's and the WTO's system of remedies in the event of treaty infringement, the EU's experience with financial compliance inducements could be a source of inspiration for the WTO membership.

D. Concluding remarks

The overview sketched out above reveals the following picture. Under general public international law, compliance is the preferred remedy following the breach of a treaty obligation, but no further inducements have been articulated to ensure that countries will comply with the ruling of a tribunal that they have breached a treaty obligation. In the WTO dispute settlement system too, compliance is the preferred remedy.

---

[62] See the Commission's Communication of 2005 [SEC (2005) 1658] <http://ec.europa.eu/eu_law/docs/docs_infringements/sec_2005_1658_en.pdf>, and of 2010 [SEC (2010) 1371 on the implementation of Article 260TFEU: <http://ec.europa.eu/eu_law/docs/docs_infringements/sec_2010_1371_en.pdf>. One observer found that the European Court of Justice followed the Commission's methodology more in respect of the calculation of penalty payments than in respect of lump sums. Jack, *id.*, 83. The Commission published an update of its calculus of lump sums and penalty payments in Communication [C(2014) 6767]: <http://ec.europa.eu/atwork/applying-eu-law/docs/c_2014_6767_en.pdf> (visited 27 June 2015).

[63] For the leading judgment see CJEU, Cases C-6/90 and C-9/90, *Francovich*, [1991] ECR I-5357.

[64] E.g., CJEU, Case C-387/97 *Commission v Greece* (2000) ECR I-5047; CJEU, C-278/01 *Commission v Spain* (2003) ECR I-14144.

Attempts to encourage or justify "efficient breaches" of WTO or public international law are misguided.

By explicitly providing for an inducement to comply with a dispute settlement ruling and the underlying treaty obligation, through retaliation, the WTO system has gone a step further than public international law generally. That in itself is to be welcomed. Retaliation consists of the imposition of additional, proportionate restrictions on the imports of goods and services from the infringing country, and/or in the suspension of certain elements of intellectual property protection. The problem is that such retaliatory measures have all kinds of disadvantages: smaller, developing countries practically have no means of crafting retaliation that impresses a large country and will induce it to comply; with retaliatory restrictions a country easily shoots in the foot; new restrictions are also unpredictable and undermine a rule-based system.

In another respect WTO law differs from general public international law as well. Should full compliance (restitution) not be feasible, in public international law it is normally envisaged that the injured country will receive compensation from the country infringing its treaty obligations. In contrast, the WTO system really offers no meaningful compensation to countries and constituents that are injured by WTO-inconsistent measures. To begin with, there is no requirement to offer restitution, that is for the WTO-infringing country to make the injured country whole for any injuries it has suffered. The WTO dispute settlement system is prospective only; it only looks to remedial action for the future. Furthermore, to the extent it makes provision for additional concessions on other goods or services (or intellectual property) to be offered by the infringing country as temporary compensation, while the infringement continues, this has proven to be a theoretical option only, which is practically never followed in practice.

Instead, the imposition of retaliatory restrictions by the prevailing country is usually considered the next step when compliance is not forthcoming. Yet retaliation does nothing to alleviate the damage done by the infringing country to exported goods or services or inadequately protected intellectual property originating in the prevailing country – neither for the past, nor for the future.

III. Why is adding the remedy of financial payments beneficial for the WTO system?

Financial payments can be an inducement for the offending country to comply, while offering a way of compensating the aggrieved countries (if not their affected private sector) – without the drawbacks of retaliatory trade restrictions (increasing unpredictability in the trading system;

self-inflicting wounds on the retaliating country; hurting innocent bystanders in the offending WTO-member).

A. *Adding pressure*

Like painful retaliatory trade restrictions, the obligation to make substantial financial payments to aggrieved countries can also induce the offending WTO member to comply. "It is the budget, stupid."

B. *Eliminating costs of retaliation*

By imposing retaliatory trade restrictions the offended WTO-country often shoots itself in the foot; imposing new import restrictions is normally prejudicial to a country's economic welfare (they produce dead-weight losses).[65] This is of particular concern to developing countries in a developmental stage.[66] In contrast, financial payments inflict no wounds on the receiving country that is aggrieved by a WTO-violation.

In this connection, we take issue with a point made in Pauwelyn's otherwise splendid analysis of retaliation.[67] He reasons that it is inherent in any form of retaliation or punishment, which seeks to induce compliance, that the retaliating government incurs a cost. Moreover, retaliation or punishment normally is unable to compensate the actual victims of the rule infringement. In support of this argument reference is made to the cost sustained by governments when putting offenders in prison. He therefore posits that one should not criticize the WTO remedy of trade retaliation too harshly.

However, the more relevant analogy here would be the financial payments offending countries can be ordered to pay when they infringe a treaty rule. Ordering such financial payments imposes very little cost on the prosecuting government; and such payments may not only induce compliance, but can be used to bring some relief to the private or public interest that has been damaged as well. In other words, we maintain our strong criticism of trade retaliation, which imposes self-inflicting wounds and can offer no relief (except in the most unusual, and unpredictable circumstances) to the damaged sectors in the retaliating country.

---

[65] Gene M. Grossmann & Alan O. Sykes, "'Optimal' Retaliation in the WTO: a commentary on the *Upland Cotton* Arbitration", 10 *World Trade Review* (2011), 133-164, at 151.

[66] Petros C. Mavroidis, "Briefing paper on Compliance in the WTO: Enforcement amongst unequal disputants", No. 4/2012, *CUTS International*, 2.

[67] Pauwelyn, above n 45, 57.

C. Promoting a rule-based trade system

Fundamentally, retaliatory trade restrictions run counter to the tenets of a rule-based, liberal trading system. They aggravate the unpredictability in the international economic environment created by WTO violations, by adding even more unforeseen trade restrictions or suspensions of internationally protected intellectual property rights. A system that relies on increased unpredictability to further its aims is not rule-based, and cannot inspire confidence amongst its constituents. In contrast, financial payments do not create similar unpredictability in the international economic environment.

D. Avoiding disadvantages for innocent by-standers in the offending Member

More particularly, in order to exercise pressure, retaliatory trade restrictions usually hurt "innocent bystanders" in the offending WTO-member. These restrictions are a particularly crude way of exercising pressure on the offending country. Expressed differently, while inducing an offending WTO-member to comply with a ruling in itself is desirable, this does not mean of course that any method of inducement is equally acceptable (the end does not justify all means). The budgetary burden of financial payments is more equally shared amongst all citizens in the offending WTO-country than the costs of trade restrictions.

Retaliatory trade restrictions may, in fact, create claims for financial payments from innocent bystanders (exporters affected by retaliatory trade restrictions) against their own, offending country.[68] From this perspective too, the payment of financial payments directly to the offended country is preferable as (i) trade flows will not be impeded, and (ii) financial payments will be paid to the country immediately damaged by the WTO-illegal restriction, rather than to companies damaged in the "second degree" in the offending WTO member.

E. Potential benefits for specific aggrieved sectors

In contrast to trade retaliation, money paid to the aggrieved WTO-country *can* be used for the benefit of its sectors suffering from the WTO-inconsistent measure. For example, in one of the first cases where an offending WTO-country volunteered to pay money, the US agreed to make a lump sum payment of $3.3 million covering three years of

---

[68]   Marco Bronckers & Sophie Goelen, "Financial Liability of the EU for WTO Violations – A legislative proposal benefiting innocent bystanders", 39 *Legal Issues of Economic Integration* (2012), 399-418.

non-compliance (2001-2004) to a fund set up by the performing rights societies in the EU, for the general assistance to their members and the promotion of author's rights.[69] Similarly, and rather more significantly, the US has agreed to make payments totaling $750 million (starting in 2010) to a fund set up for the Brazilian Cotton Institute for technical assistance and capacity building for Brazil's cotton sector,[70] for as long as it did not implement the WTO's condemnation of US subsidies to its cotton industry.

It is noteworthy that in both cases the offending WTO member stipulated that the money could not be paid directly to the affected private stakeholders in the aggrieved country. One can imagine the reluctance of the offending government to subsidize a foreign industry, when the payments are substantial. This could be seen to undermine the policy of the very measure that was declared WTO-illegal to begin with, and which the WTO-member is not prepared to withdraw.[71] And when the payments are modest, finding an equitable distribution mechanism for the receiving country may be too cumbersome. In such cases, an intermediary fund as was used in the two cases mentioned here can provide useful assistance to the private sector concerned in the aggrieved WTO member.

In other words, although the WTO dispute settlement system presently makes no provision for reparation in the public international law sense, we submit that adding some measure of compensation is a useful addition to the WTO's toolbox. This is especially true for developing countries, whose entire economies can be seriously disrupted by WTO-illegal measures. The examples of *EC Bananas*, *EC Sugar* and *US Cotton* come to mind.[72]

---

[69] Financial payments do not always achieve the goal of compliance. As of this writing, the United States still has not implemented the WTO ruling at issue: WTO Panel Report *United States – Section 110(5) of the US Copyright Act*, WT/DS160/R, adopted 15 June 2000. Of course, the payment offered in this case was so small that the United States hardly felt any budgetary pressure. Rebecca Ullman, "Enhancing the WTO Tool Kit: the Case for Financial Compensation", 9 *Richmond Journal of Global Law and Business* 2 (2010) 167-97.

[70] For the latest instalment of $300 million see *United States – Subsidies on Upland Cotton*, WT/DS267/46 (23 October 2014). The total amount of $750 million in US payments to the Brazilian Cotton Institute was mentioned in Alex Lawson, "International Trade Group Of The Year: Sidley Austin", *Law 360* (January 26, 2015): <http://www.law360.com/articles/614886/international-trade-group-of-the-year-sidley-austin>.

[71] Davies, above n 57, at 64-66.

[72] WTO Appellate Body Report, *EC – Regime for the Importation, Sale and Distribution of Bananas*, WT/DS27/AB/R, adopted 9 September 1997; WTO Appellate Body Report, *EC – Export Subsidies on Sugar*, WT/DS265/AB/R, WT/DS266/AB/R, WT/DS283/AB/R, adopted 28 April 2005; WTO Appellate Body Report, *United States – Subsidies on Upland Cotton*, WT/DS267/R, adopted 21 March 2005.

F. Opposing gamesmanship

As already indicated, the WTO's dispute settlement system is prospective in nature, in that WTO members found to have violated WTO rules presently do not have to worry about the past.[73] This distinguishing feature has been welcomed for various reasons. It would notably encourage WTO members to take on new obligations to liberalize trade, or to follow multilateral governance principles, more easily. Members would also have to worry less about the consequences of good faith violations. And there might be something special about the nature of WTO rules, being more about obligations regarding results than about conduct.[74] We do not see anything specific in WTO rules, compared to other international (economic) agreements, that would not make them amenable to retroactive remedies in dispute settlement. Yet we are sensitive to the more pragmatic concern that full retroactivity would be a disincentive to the membership to develop WTO rules, given that on the international plane the WTO dispute settlement process is remarkably rigorous.

However, it is one thing to advocate that the remedies of WTO dispute settlement system should not be fully retroactive; it is quite another thing to condone strategic gamesmanship of WTO members, who institute or maintain WTO-illegal measures in the knowledge that they run no risk for the duration of WTO dispute settlement proceedings, to which a "reasonable" period of implementation can be added. Gamesmanship or foot-dragging is a serious weakness of WTO dispute settlement in its current state. When critics are saying that WTO dispute settlement takes too long, they are really not complaining about the length of the process – in relation to other international procedures and to most domestic litigation the WTO's time table compares favorably (even if the deadlines imposed by the DSU have been slipping, notably at the panel stage)[75]. The critical point is that at the end of the few years which the process takes, the WTO pays no mind to the past. This is unusual compared to other litigation, and severely limits the benefit of a successful challenge for a complainant.

Expressed differently, the temptation for WTO members faced with an awkward domestic problem to accept the risk of WTO litigation, as they only need to worry about the consequences later, is strong. Some

---

[73] See above n 45.

[74] For a recent rehearsal of the arguments in favor of the prospective nature of WTO remedies see Claus D. Zimmerman, "The Neglected Link Between the Legal Nature of WTO Rules, the Political Filtering of WTO Disputes, and the Absence of Retrospective WTO Remedies", 4 *Trade, Law & Development* 1 (2012) 251-62.

[75] See William J. Davey, "WTO dispute settlement: promise fulfilled?", in Inge Govaere, Reinhard Quick, Marco Bronckers, (eds.), *Trade and Competition Law in the EU and Beyond* (Edward Elgar 2011) 194-203, at 200-01.

brake on foot-dragging could therefore be usefully added to the system, by stipulating that financial liability starts to run from the day a request for WTO consultations, or for the establishment of a WTO panel, is filed. As from this moment onwards, having been put on notice that and why its conduct is problematic in WTO legal terms, it becomes more difficult for a defendant country to maintain that it committed WTO violations in good faith. And again, given that the receipt of financial payments, contrary to the imposition of retaliatory restrictions, imposes no deadweight losses, cutting back on the prospective nature of WTO dispute settlement rulings in this way raises no concern for the economy of the prevailing country.[76]

G. *Equally beneficial to small and/or developing Members*

One also must also recognize that, certainly in relation to (large) developed countries, (small) developing countries have no effective means of retaliation; their markets are simply too small to make an impression (recall Ecuador in *EC Bananas* and Antigua and Barbuda in *US Gambling*).[77] Providing more effective compliance inducements and some reparation of damages to developing countries can also add a measure of "fairness" to the WTO legal system.[78] This will enhance the legitimacy of the organization, and its appeal as an agent of global governance.

IV. Why are the objections to financial payments unpersuasive?

A. *No regime change*

According to some commentators, giving the power to WTO tribunals to impose financial penalties on governments would transform the nature of the WTO system, and might "constitutionalize" WTO

---

[76] Compare Grossman & Sykes, above n 63, at 151 (who worry about foot-dragging but are reluctant to allow any form of retroactivity in the remedies of WTO dispute settlement as they admit only classic trade retaliation, with the accompanying negative effect of deadweight losses on the retaliating country).

[77] WTO Decision by the Arbitrators, *EC – Regime for the Importation, Sale and Distribution of Bananas – Recourse to Arbitration by the EC under Article 22.6 of the DSU*, WT/DS27/ARB/ECU, adopted 24 March 2000, paras. 73, 126 and 177; WTO Decision by the Arbitrators, *United States – Measures Affecting the Cross-Border Supply of Gambling and Betting Services, Recourse to Arbitration by Antigua and Barbuda under Article 22.6 of the DSU*, WT/DS285/ARB, adopted 21 December 2007, para. 4.114; The Australian (online edition), *WTO approves Antigua sanctions on US* (29 January 2013).

[78] Bronckers & Van den Broek, above n 4, at 111.

rules. This hesitation points to an underlying unease about the WTO system. Perhaps the rules of the WTO are not sufficiently clear or robust so that countries found to "violate" them ought not to be exposed to rigorous sanctions. In this view, retaliation to induce compliance at some point in the future, without regard to the past, may appear sufficiently "soft" while financial penalties would be too harsh.

However, the idea that retaliation is a substantially softer remedy than financial penalties is misplaced. Just imagine the damage that retaliatory restrictions inflict on companies from the WTO offending country. Depending on the importance of the market in the retaliating country, this may inflict serious losses on those companies or even force them into bankruptcy. It is not because the offending country under the present WTO-system is able to shift these costs onto its unsuspecting companies or citizens, rather than assuming a financial penalty on its budget, that the countermeasure authorized by a WTO tribunal is less harsh.

Now one might perceive a financial penalty to be paid by a sovereign nation to be more delicate than a financial loss (resulting from retaliation) inflicted on an ordinary citizen. But is this really a meaningful distinction in the WTO-system, where many cases brought by governments involve competing private interests on both sides? Furthermore, speaking about perceptions, the authorization of retaliatory restrictions represents the temporary suspension or roll-back of WTO obligations by the retaliating country. From a WTO-systemic perspective this is rather more problematic than the introduction of financial remedies.

As financial penalties are not fundamentally harsher than regulatory restrictions, there is also no good reason to think that the introduction of financial remedies would somehow constitutionalize WTO rules. If a WTO member believes that it cannot comply with a particular WTO-ruling, at least for a while, a system of financial remedies will still allow this Member to make this choice. Yet, rather than shifting the cost of this choice onto only some of its citizens (as would be the case with retaliation) the Member would have to assume these costs on its budget, which would then become an expense for the public at large.

There is also no reason to think that WTO rules are fundamentally less clear or not as robustly formulated as other (international) rules. It is true, as with most bodies of rules, that some infringements of WTO law are more obvious than others. Yet it is entirely possible when imposing a financial penalty (as when framing other remedies, such as retaliation, one might add) for a WTO tribunal to differentiate according to the seriousness of the infringement. Again, the practice in the EU provides good illustrations as to how might this might work.[79]

---

[79]   See text above at note 60.

B. Realistic remedy

One objection is that financial payments do not appear to be a realistic remedy, as a country that refuses to implement a WTO-ruling can also be expected to refuse to pay financial payments. Hence, it is argued that the positive effect of introducing monetary payments into the dispute settlement system – if any – is likely to remain small. More particularly, the benefits, if any, of a reform of the retaliation regime would not be worth the political capital invested by developing countries.[80] The experience under public international law, analyzed above, shows that this prediction is unfounded. Countries that are ordered to pay financial awards following a treaty violation usually comply.[81]

By way of further illustration,[82] one could add here that EU Member States have effectively paid the financial penalties imposed on them by the European Court for not complying with EU law as well.[83] Although details are not readily available, the EU annual budgets indicate for example that from 2005 until 2009 three Member States (i.e., France, Greece, Portugal) paid almost €100 million in total in seven infringement cases.[84] Furthermore, the practice with FTAs, supposedly a testing ground for how a multilateral system like the WTO might evolve, also suggests that monetary relief is considered a useful (additional) remedy for treaty violations. Thus, recent FTAs negotiated by the United States envisage monetary compensation in the event of treaty violations.[85]

---

[80] Bohanes & Garza, above n 6, at 101.

[81] See above text notes 13-24.

[82] See above n 18-21.

[83] See above n 67-71.

[84] See <http://ec.europa.eu/budget/biblio/documents/2013/2013_en.cfm> (visited 22 June 2015).

[85] Kyle Bagwell, "Remedies in the World Trade Organization: an Economic Perspective", in Merit E. Janow, Victoria Donaldson & Alan Yanovich (eds.), *The WTO: Governance, Dispute Settlement, and Developing Countries* (Juris Publishing 2008), 733-70, at 751. Recent examples of such a provision can be found in Art. 21.16 of the US – Colombia FTA (signed 22 November 2006, entered into force 15 May 2012), Art. 22.13 of the US – South Korea FTA (signed 30 June 2007, entered into force 15 March 2012), Art. 21.16 of the US – Peru Trade Promotion Agreement [TPA] (signed 12 April 2007, entered into force 1 February 2009) or Art. 20.11 of the Oman – US FTA (signed 19 January 2006, entered into force 1 January 2009). In the EU FTAs however, such policy has not yet been adopted. For example, Art. 107 of the EU – Central America Association Agreement stipulates that "[a] Party applying a bilateral safeguard measure shall consult with the Party whose products are subject to the measure in order to mutually agree on appropriate trade liberalising compensation in the form of concessions having substantially equivalent trade effect" (signed 29 June 2012, not entered into force yet). Similar provisions can be found in Art. 54 of the EU – Peru/ Colombia FTA (signed 26 June 2012, entered into force 1 March 2013 with regard to Peru; not yet with regard to Colombia) and Art. 3.4 of the EU – South Korea FTA (signed 6 October 2010, entered into force 1 July 2011).

Once the principle of financial remedies is accepted in the WTO, one could think of further refinements or "confidence-building measures". For example, suppose that following the introduction of financial payments in the WTO, the record would come to show that (contrary to the experiences in public international law) WTO Members would not pay the amounts imposed on them by WTO tribunals. At that point a system of bonds could be introduced, which (developed) countries would post up front. In an actual dispute, (developing) countries could draw on these bonds if and when a WTO-offending Member would not comply with a ruling.[86] This system of bonds would then alleviate uncertainty that a WTO Member might not execute the financial penalty it was ordered to pay by a WTO tribunal.

C. Suitable remedy

It is also questioned whether financial payments actually fit the objective of inducing compliance. Do financial payments not allow the offending country to "buy itself out of an infringement"– and would this remedy not favor rich countries, which have the means to buy allowances to violate their obligations?

A particular concern in this regard has been raised by the significant payments made by the United States to Brazil, currently estimated to the tune of some \$750 million, in lieu of compliance with the WTO ruling which condemned US subsidies to its cotton industry.[87] To the extent these payments take on the character of a permanent settlement of the dispute, they are pernicious. They do not benefit other (e.g., African) producers of cotton, which continue to be prejudiced by distortive US cotton subsidies. Furthermore, such a permanent settlement signals that the WTO system also in other cases may be open to what at least some of the Members would consider "efficient breaches".[88] Rather than revealing welcome flexibility of the WTO's remedies, such settlements contribute to the breakdown of the WTO's rule-based system.[89]

However, to the extent financial penalties are substantial and recurring, they send the message that compliance is the ultimate goal. This message would be strengthened if the penalties would increase further in the event non-compliance continued for a longer period of time. Furthermore,

---

[86] Nuno Limao and Kamal Saggi, "Size Inequality, Coordination Externalities and International Trade agreements", 63 *European Economic Review* (2013), 10-27.

[87] See text, *supra*, at note 70.

[88] See text, *supra*, at note 57.

[89] See text, *supra*, at note 58. For another critique of the *Upland Cotton* settlement see Simon Evenett & Alejandro Jara, "Settling WTO disputes without solving the problem: Abusing compensation", *Vox* (9 December 2014) <http://www.voxeu.org/article/settling-wto-disputes-without-solving-problem-abusing-compensation>.

when the amount of the payments takes into the account the offending country's ability to pay (as the EU does by referring to a country's GDP in setting penalties), rich countries need not be favored.

D. Inter-state remedy

Various objections have also been raised against financial payments by an offending WTO Member to affected private industries or sectors in the aggrieved country. Such an action would go beyond what is proposed in this paper, although we would leave the possibility open for the complaining government to distribute the payments among its damaged industries – a discussion which the Appellate Body in the *Upland Cotton* case for example was keen to avoid. This would be a change from the current system, which decouples the trade sanctions from the exporters who suffer from the WTO violation.[90] If affected industries knew they would be financially compensated in the event a WTO Member were found to violate WTO law, some observers have raised concern that industries might "overinvest" in WTO rules.[91] We have difficulty accepting this concern, as it contradicts a key element of a rule-based system, which is precisely to create a more predictable environment so as to encourage private parties to "invest" in international transactions and create more economic welfare. Why should there be a limit to this "investment", and where is the line to be drawn?

Similarly, we also do not share the concern that the introduction of financial payments would lead to an unwelcome increase in WTO litigation spurred on by private interest groups.[92] First, the expectation of a country that instituting or maintaining WTO-illegal measures may create financial exposure down the line could lead to greater rule compliance to begin with, without any litigation taking place. Second, it would be a positive vote of confidence in the WTO system, in the event private stakeholders and especially smaller, developing countries would bring more cases to the WTO on the grounds that, faced with a non-complying country, they would have access to a remedy that actually offers some benefit to them.

Another concern is that the difficulty of calculating damages would increase, when moving from an aggregate analysis to the level of individual private parties.[93] As has been pointed out, this is a practical difficulty that surely can be overcome by developing expertise. Furthermore, the calculations which have to be undertaken to calculate the "equivalent"

---

[90]   See generally, Sykes, above n 5.
[91]   *Id.*, at 350-51.
[92]   *Id.*, at 352.
[93]   *Id.*, at 351.

level of trade concessions that can be withdrawn as a retaliatory measure also implies a considerable amount of complexity.[94] This problem would not be as pressing in any event in case one would follow our proposal and not have the ambition of calculating the damages suffered to the private sector more or less precisely in each and every case.

Admittedly, it may not be easy conceptually to distinguish the adverse impact of a WTO violation on states over and above the adverse impact on private entities.[95] However, in our view financial payments in the WTO's governmental dispute settlement system would not only be about the compensation of damages but also have the objective of inducing compliance (while keeping in mind the ability to pay of the offending country). Such a system will not lead to either excessive or insufficient compensation of damages, as private damages do not exclusively determine the financial payments.[96] The methodology used by the EU in calculating financial sanctions in the event of non-compliance by Member States illustrates how this might work.

Indeed, one ought to recall our starting point: we are discussing financial payments as a remedy in government-to-government disputes, rather than as a remedy targeted to private actors in a kind of investor-state arbitration system. In the latter case, determining adequate compensation for the private investor is the overriding objective. Yet in the case of government-to-government disputes in the setting of the WTO, rule compliance is the prime concern. The damage suffered by the private sector can help guide the amount that is to be paid, but it is not decisive – especially where recurring financial payments are concerned that seek to induce compliance. Furthermore, it is up to the receiving government to assess how and to what extent the financial payments are to be distributed amongst its private sector damaged by the foreign WTO-illegal measure.

E. Affordable remedy

Another objection sometimes raised is that offending developing countries could not afford to make financial payments to an aggrieved WTO member. However, this is too sweeping a statement. It is increasingly recognized that there are important distinctions within the

---

[94] Bagwell, above n 85, at 752. This is also illustrated by the critical case study of the retaliation authorized in the recent *Upland Cotton* dispute in Grossman & Sykes, above n 65.

[95] Davies, above n 57, at 47.

[96] Sykes, above n 5, at 352. In fairness, Sykes was responding here to Bronckers & van den Broek's analogy of such fixed amounts to the notion of "liquidated damages". See Bronckers & Van den Broek, above n 4, at 113-14. That terminology invites a reflection of how such amounts would relate to actual damages.

group of countries commonly referred to as "developing". As opposed to the exclusion of all developing countries from this remedy, the better approach would be to explicitly recognize the ability to pay (reflected, for instance, in GDP) as an important factor in the calculation of financial payments, even though this may add a measure of complexity to the exercise.[97] Furthermore, by taking into account the seriousness of the breach, one could also address the concern that particularly in technically complex cases developing countries (given a relative lack of knowhow and resources) may more easily commit breaches of WTO law in good faith.[98] In fact, if good faith breaches are made less expensive this could be an encouragement for the WTO membership at large to assume new liberalization or governance obligations in the WTO.[99] Again, the model developed in the EU for the calculation of financial sanctions against non-complying Member States provides a useful illustration.

F. Difficult but Doable

We are not pretending that "financial" remedies will easily or soon be introduced. Powerful players in the WTO, including the EU, seem rather comfortable with the current system. Yet this does not mean that their present comfort is acceptable, or immune to change.

Thus, for the EU, which sees itself as a major supporter of the WTO, it is dubious policy to resist a reform of remedies which effectively are unavailable to a large number of WTO members, notably developing countries. Also from a domestic perspective it is deplorable that the EU apparently prefers to be exposed to retaliation from third countries (as it was in the *Hormones* and *Bananas* retaliation by the United States) than to bear the burden of paying financial penalties to aggrieved third countries for as long as the EU cannot bring itself into compliance with its WTO obligations. Rather than making the cost of its non-compliance visible to all as an expenditure on its budget, and thereby elicit a public debate about its policy choice not to comply with a WTO ruling, the EU shifts the cost of its non-compliance rather less visibly to individual EU companies who have to bear the brunt of retaliatory restrictions imposed by third countries. Regrettably, the European Court of Justice to date has endorsed the cynical refusal of the EU institutions to honor demands of those European industries to be compensated for the damage they suffer as a result of such retaliatory restrictions abroad, because of WTO disputes in which they have no stake.[100]

---

[97] Compare the analyses of the capacity to pay in Michael Waibel, *Sovereign Defaults before International Courts and Tribunals* (Cambridge University Press 2011).

[98] Zimmerman, above n 74, at 255.

[99] Compare, above n 73-75.

[100] Bronckers and Goelen, above, n 68.

The victims of these dubious policies (developing countries; domestic industries) may well create a dynamic to force change on hitherto complacent WTO members. Further experiences with financial penalties in FTAs may also reduce the resistance to a reform of WTO remedies.[101] It is difficult to predict when the time will be ripe for such a change. But the WTO's own history shows that fundamental change can and does come. Who would have thought in the 1970s or 1980s, when the GATT's consensus-based system seemed to break down,[102] that with the WTO's establishment in 1994 a compulsory, two-tiered and time-limited dispute settlement mechanism would emerge?

V. Proposal

The main elements of our proposal could be summarized as follows:

A. Calculating payments

Financial payments would be calculated with a view to inducing compliance with a WTO rule. The starting amount could vary depending on the seriousness of the infringement, and on the injury inflicted by the transgression. A hierarchy of norms has been introduced in the FTAs concluded by the US, for example, in that the compensation procedure becomes stricter where the violation relates to environmental or labor laws.[103] As far as WTO rules go, a violation of the MFN principle could weigh more heavily, for instance, than the improper valuation of imported goods for the assessment of customs duties. A precise calculation of damages would not be necessary, as the inducement to comply with the WTO ruling rather than compensation is the primary objective here. Any amount thus calculated could be tempered (or increased) by the offending country's ability to pay, which could be assessed by reference to its GNP.

One model for calculations that could be looked at is the methodology the European Commission has developed with regard to EU Treaty infringement proceedings, applying periodic penalty payments and lump sum payments with the foremost goal to induce EU Member States compliance, rather than repair damage.[104] The level of these recurring

---

[101] See above, text at n 85.
[102] John H. Jackson, "The Crumbling Institutions of the Liberal Trade system", 12 *Journal of World Trade* (1978), 93-106.
[103] Davies, above n 57, at 40.
[104] See text above at notes 61-62.

financial payments could be established, like the level of retaliatory suspension of concessions at present, by a separate panel decision.[105]

B. Term of payments

An inducement to comply requires that recurring payments would continue for as long the state of non-compliance lasts. Compliance would be further encouraged if such recurring payments would increase the longer the state of non-compliance persists. The possibility of such an increase could be limited to serious infringements.

C. Retro-activity of payments

In order to counter the problem of gamesmanship, a lump sum could be added for the past in addition to recurring penalty payments for the continuation of the infringement in the future. Lump sums will amplify the message to recalcitrant Members that foot-dragging to comply with WTO law comes at a cost. Furthermore, a lump sum can also offer some redress (reparation) for the past. If one does not want to give full retroactive effect to a WTO-ruling, the lump sum might be related to the period of infringement between the request for WTO-consultations or for the establishment of a panel, and the date on which a WTO tribunal imposed recurring financial payments in order to induce the offending country to comply with its ruling. One factor to calculate such a lump sum could be the nature of infringement: in the event of WTO-illegal taxes, customs, antidumping or countervailing duties, for example, the financial payment might equal the amount of wrongfully levied duties (minus any reimbursement already given by the offending country to importers under its domestic law). Again, the methodology which the EU Commission has elaborated in connection with EU Treaty infringements can be a starting point for reflections within the WTO membership.

In order to deter foot-dragging even more effectively, provision could be made for the payment of lump sums together with a finding that a WTO Member has infringed its WTO commitments. In other words, whenever a WTO Member is found to have violated its WTO commitments it would be liable to pay some amount to the aggrieved country, notably depending on the nature of the infringement and its ability to pay. If the offending country did not bring itself into compliance within a reasonable period of time, the offending Member would in addition become liable for recurring financial payments to the aggrieved country to induce compliance.

---

[105] DSU Art. 22 (6).

D. Beneficiary of payments

Financial payments would be made by an offending country to an aggrieved country (or to a private fund or entity designated by the aggrieved country). Expressed differently, as a matter of WTO law the private sector affected by a WTO-violation would derive no direct claim to such financial payments – the distribution of such payments would be left to the aggrieved countries receiving the payments.

VI. Conclusion

In our view the primary objective of WTO dispute settlement is that Members who have been found to infringe their WTO obligations bring themselves into compliance. This is in keeping with the central element of WTO dispute settlement, which is to provide "*security and predictability*" to the multilateral trading system.[106] It is fundamentally inconsistent with these tenets to propose, as some have done, that WTO members should have the choice of continuing to breach their WTO obligations if they would deem the payment of compensation to complaining Members to be more "efficient" than compliance.

Under general public international law too compliance is the preferred remedy following the breach of a treaty obligation, but no further inducements have been articulated to ensure that countries will comply with the ruling of a tribunal that they have breached a treaty obligation. By explicitly providing for an inducement to comply with a dispute settlement ruling and the underlying treaty obligation, through retaliation, the WTO system has gone a step further than public international law generally, and that in itself is to be welcomed. The problem is that retaliatory measures have all kinds of disadvantages: smaller, developing countries practically have no means of crafting retaliation that impresses a large country and will induce it to comply; with retaliatory restrictions a country easily shoots in the foot; new restrictions are also unpredictable and undermine a rule-based system.

In another respect WTO law differs from general public international law as well. Should full compliance (restitution) not be feasible, in public international law it is normally envisaged that the injured country will receive compensation from the country infringing its treaty obligations. In contrast, the WTO system really offers no meaningful compensation to countries and constituents that are injured by WTO-inconsistent measures. To begin with, there is no requirement to offer restitution; that is for the WTO-infringing country to make the injured country whole

---

[106] DSU Art. 3 (2).

for any injuries it has suffered. The WTO dispute settlement is deemed prospective only. Furthermore, to the extent it makes provision for additional concessions on other goods or services (or intellectual property) to be offered by the infringing country as temporary compensation for the future, while the infringement continues, this has proven to be a theoretical option only, which is practically never followed in practice. Instead, the imposition of retaliatory restrictions by the prevailing country is usually considered the next step when compliance is not forthcoming. Yet retaliation does nothing to alleviate the damage done by the infringing country to exported goods or services or inadequately protected intellectual property – neither for the past, nor for the future.

When looking for improvements to the present WTO system, the first thing to consider would be an alternative mechanism to induce compliance. We submit that financial payments offer several advantages: the obligation to pay a substantial amount of money can be a strong incentive for countries large and small to comply with rulings and the underlying rules; such payments can be tailored to the seriousness of the infringement, as well as the infringing country's ability to pay; and a payment obligation does not impinge on the prevailing country's interests, nor does it undermine the rules-based system. Like the WTO, the EU as well goes further than general public international law in making provision for compliance inducements following treaty infringements. Some twenty years ago the EU system added financial payments as a remedy, and its experience can be a source of inspiration for the WTO membership.

Another consideration is that such financial payments, while not designed to offset the damage caused by a WTO-infringing measure, as a matter of fact do offer a measure of financial compensation to the prevailing country. In keeping with the government-to-government nature of WTO dispute settlement it should be left to the government receiving the payments whether and how it wants to distribute such payments to the private sector(s) adversely affected by the WTO-infringing measure.

To sceptics who doubt that WTO Members ordered to make financial payments will do so we point to the experience in public international law. The record shows that countries found to have violated their international obligations and being ordered to pay financial reparation usually comply. Why would this be different in the WTO? Furthermore, it is of interest that in a series of recent bilateral trade agreements, notably those to which the United States is a party, provision for financial remedies is being made.

We also recommend to modify the prospective nature of WTO dispute settlement somewhat, in that financial liability would start from the moment the request for consultations or a panel has been made. The defendant country is then put on notice that its measure is problematic under WTO law. This is a necessary step to counter foot-dragging in implementing WTO obligations, which is presently a serious weakness of the WTO system.

The introduction of financial payments will not resolve all problems associated with the WTO dispute settlement system, such as the impact of power asymmetries. By emphasizing that financial payments can be a better inducement to compliance than trade retaliation, we also do not underestimate compliance incentives outside the remedies offered by the WTO dispute settlement system, such as the reputational or "community" costs an offending member incurs.[107] But we are convinced that the introduction of financial payments will bring notable benefits to the current system and its members.

Furthermore, we realize of course that the WTO dispute settlement system represents a delicate balance between what might be good for the system and what Members are willing to accept. Accordingly, we would recommend starting out modestly, or pragmatically, so as not to upset this balance too much. For example, despite our misgivings about the current remedy of trade retaliation, we would not abandon this remedy immediately but, in a first stage, add financial payments as an alternative. Prevailing countries would be left with the choice to retaliate or to request financial payments as an inducement on the losing country to comply. Some years of experience should help to demonstrate that financial payments are fit to replace retaliation. Experience can also indicate what, if any, modalities need to be introduced in this remedy to make it work satisfactorily.

***

---

[107] Pauwelyn, above n 45, at 59.

A Comment

Bernard HOEKMAN[1]

A central feature of the dispute settlement system of the WTO is that the remedies that are available are limited. Adjudicating bodies will generally rule that a State that is not in compliance with its obligations take measures to do so. If the WTO member concerned does not do so the affected government will be authorized to take retaliatory measures. The WTO does not call on its members to take collective action nor is there any scope to exclude a country from any or all benefits that accrue as a result of membership. Thus, as has often been observed in the literature on the WTO, ultimately the WTO is (has to be) a self-enforcing agreement, with (the threat of) retaliation as the only mechanism available to respond to actions by a member that violates its commitments. Bronckers and Baetens argue that it is possible and desirable to change the menu of options to ensure compliance with negotiated WTO obligations. Based on a discussion of prevailing remedy systems under general public international law and those available in the EU, they argue in favor of introducing the possibility of financial payments as a remedy into WTO dispute settlement and outline how this might be done in practice.

From an economic perspective there is much to be said for the approach that is proposed by the authors. Economists have long recognized that there are major downsides associated with retaliation as an enforcement mechanism. These include the fact that retaliation entails additional costs for the country taking action, which comes on top of the harm done by non-compliance on the part of the trading partner, and that this reduces the credibility (effectiveness) of the retaliatory threat. Moreover, small countries are unlikely to be able to impose "enough pain" on a large state to induce it to comply with the rulings on a panel or the Appellate Body. Economists have pointed out that more efficient instruments can be identified in principle, including compensation of the affected trading party (parties) by the offending state. Thus, the proposition advocated by the authors is one that economists would agree with. The problems associated with retaliation are well known and have been raised repeatedly over the years by delegations representing developing countries in Geneva.

---

[1]   Professor at the European University Institute and CPR Research Fellow.

The paper does a good job of summarizing the various arguments against retaliation as an instrument. One of these is that it does not help the exporting firms who are negatively affected by a violation, unless these firms also sell domestically and the retaliation targets imports of competing products from the country that does not comply. The likelihood of such "balancing" is low. While this is a valid argument, the broader issue here is that governments do not appear to want to help the affected firms. Even if countries limit enforcement to retaliation it is possible for the retaliating government to assist its negatively affected exporters. Retaliation will generally involve raising tariffs on a set of goods imported from the non-complying nation. This generates revenue. This could be used to compensate the industry that has lost from the violation. While consumers end up paying the price and retaliation is inefficient from a welfare perspective, the overall cost to each consumer may be low if the retaliation does not imply that a substantial share of the consumption bundle is affected. The point is that compensation for affected exporters is possible under the current regime. This suggests that governments are not that concerned with compensating the firms that have lost out through no fault of their own. This raises the question whether anything would change if a financial payment option was introduced into the WTO. At the end of the day it is left to the discretion of the government what it does with the funds.

A basic problem with retaliation is that it often is not effective even if the players are large. In instances where the EU and the US retaliated against each other, such as in Bananas dispute, which involved very carefully trying to select which industries and companies to target for retaliatory measures so as to maximize the political pain and pressure for compliance with WTO rulings, at the end of it is not clear that it helped much in ultimately getting the case to be resolved. But the whole process led to significant costs for affected companies and thus their workers and communities they were based in. Thus, innocent bystanders are forced to "take one for the team" in the violating country, but if governments don't particularly care about the costs that are incurred, retaliation will not work.

Turning to the financial payments dimension of the paper, I would like to raise two issues. First, from an economic efficiency point of view, financial payments are a better approach than retaliation as it avoids the deadweight costs of protection and the direct costs imposed on the innocent bystanders. The key question – aside from the issue of getting countries to agree to use payments as an (interim) remedy – is how do you design this in a way so that it is incentive compatible? The argument in the paper is primarily normative. Over simplifying, the argument is that: (i) from an effectiveness and efficiency point payments are superior to retaliation; *and* (ii) the payment option is feasible to implement in the WTO because states use payments in other contexts. That is all well and good, but what are the incentives that will induce a government to go the payments route? The incentives are to stick with retaliation – as this ensures that small countries cannot exercise credible threats. The GATT/ WTO system arguably was not designed to take care of the interests of small countries – a point argued strongly by the authors. But this raises the question why large states should go down the financial payments route? How can this be operationalized ex ante so that ex post payments are actually used?

Research by Limão and Saggi[2] concludes that a mechanism relying on payments by a country that does not comply will need to be involved in a system in which credible commitments are made *ex ante*, through for example the posting of bonds in an "escrow account". That is funds must be committed upfront. They show, moreover, that there are various technical issues that need to be addressed to make this work. One challenge may be that small countries face financial constraints that make such an ex ante financial commitment difficult. Limão and Saggi show that a system which has a combination of bonds which are pre-paid by large countries and fines which would apply to smaller countries could be designed to have the desirable effects. Thus, if there is a violation and the country concerned does not want to ("cannot") implement a ruling, a system where the large countries enforce the payment of compensation to whoever is being hurt through imposition of fines (which they can enforce because they have market power and they can ultimately retaliate) and small countries can get large countries to compensate them because the bonds have been paid up front is conceivable. There are important corollary questions such as whether posting of bonds is done so that every country is sitting on some of this money or whether a third party such as the WTO secretariat should manage this. But the main finding is that retaliation stays part of the equation in the sense that there needs to be an incentive for large countries to post the bonds. What is this incentive? Alternatively put, how would you go about convincing large countries to credibly commit to providing financial payments?

Whatever the efficiency rationale for moving to a system of payments, countries are not necessarily interested in getting payments from a country that is in violation. They want that country to comply. Giving them some money is not going to change anything. Similarly, countries are unlikely to be very willing to put significant amounts of money on the table. Thus, while one can conceptually design a system that makes sense, putting it in place is a different story. If you look at the rare instances where compensation has been paid to date it has always been between large countries – the EU, the US and Brazil. Small countries have not been compensated. This illustrates the importance of market power

---

[2]   Nuno Limão and Kamal Saggi, "Size Inequality, Coordination Externalities and International Trade Agreements", 63 *European Economic Review* (2013), 10-27.

(the credibility of retaliatory threats) and in turn suggests a necessary condition for moving towards the proposals made in the paper is that small countries organize themselves to generate such market power – e.g., through greater collective enforcement.

Summing up, it is possible to conceive of systems that are more efficient and effective that what we have at the moment, but the challenge is getting from A to B. We need to consider seriously the incentives confronting different actors. In the case of small countries, which have the greatest stake in a move away from sole reliance on retaliation, the need is to understand the constraints to collective action. Why don't small countries do more to cooperate when bringing disputes thus permitting collective threats to retaliate? These questions are directly relevant for efforts to operationalize a financial payment mechanism.

A Comment

Christian TIETJE[1]

Jacques Bourgeois invited us to strongly criticize the papers we were asked to comment on. Hence, I want to add some criticism to that of Bernard Hoekman. My comment will be more from a lawyer's perspective, and it concerns the general concept of compliance with DSB decisions.

First of all, the paper by Bronckers and Baetens starts off with an assumption that there is a general compliance problem in international law and also in WTO law. I am skeptical. I do not see that much of a compliance problem. With regard to international law in general, I strongly believe in what has been said by Louis Henkins, and you probably all know this quote: "almost all nations observe almost all principles of international law, almost all of the time".[2] This is still correct and true and it is also the reality in the WTO context. *Charzow Factory*,[3] which is of course the legal starting point for the considerations of Marco, is not normality, but rather, a pathological situation. In order to discuss the compliance structure of WTO law, however, it is necessary to analyze normality, not some pathological situation. Moreover, there is not empirical evidence from public international law proving that any financial remedy will make compliance systems better.

My thesis therefore would be that there are always multiple considerations and incentives concerning compliance by States.[4] It is thus not only financial remedies. However, before going into detail on this, it is necessary to look at the compliance record in the sense of Article 22 DSU. At the end of 2013, we had 148 panel and appellate body reports adopted. Out of these, 24 were Article 22 cases. Thus, in 16% of all cases, we had problems with compliance. And out of these 24 cases in only 10 disputes, not individual cases, but subject matters, we had an authorization of suspension of concessions, which amounts to 6.8%. Even if you round

---

[1]   Prof. Dr. Christian Tietje, LLM. Chair of Public Law, European Law and International Economic Law, Law School, University of Halle.

[2]   Louis Henkin, How Nations Behave: Law and Foreign Policy, 2nd ed., New York 1979, 47.

[3]   Germany v. Poland, (1927) P.C.I.J., Ser. A, No. 9.

[4]   For details on this and the following parts of this comment see already Christian Tietje, *The WTO Sanctions Regime and International Constitutional Political Economy – Comment*, University of Illinois Law Review 2008, 383-387.

the numbers up, we are still under 10% in this regard and that is the figure that is important. Furthermore, we have to look at the context of the cases where we had compliance problems. I will revisit this issue later.

If we compare the compliance record of the DSB with the International Court of Justice (ICJ), there is compliance in around 80% of cases before the ICJ where parties brought the case forward based on mutual consent. However, only around 50% of decisions had a positive compliance record in situations where the defending State opposed the proceedings.[5] Thus, we actually have a wonderful compliance record in WTO law, one could say. And, as I said, we also have to look at the content of the non-compliance cases, and I will return to that.

Second, it is important to be clear on why we criticize the idea of suspension of concessions. First, the rationale of the WTO model of suspension of concession is very different from the *Charzow Factory* rationale. Art. 22 DSU provides for the authorization of a suspension of concessions exclusively for the future. This means that the only concessions that may be suspended are those that are equivalent to the benefits to be expected by a suspending WTO member in the case of future non-compliance by another member. This concept is significantly different from general public international law on state responsibility that considers past as well as expected future injury.[6] Marco Bronckers has made this point in his paper.

Moreover, as Art. 22 DSU focuses exclusively on the suspension of concessions, it is important to ask what the actual rationale of such a suspension of concessions is. The notion of "concessions" is deeply rooted in the history of the world trading system, dating back to the 19th century. It essentially refers to a non-liberal, protectionist trading system based on the classical idea of mercantilism. *Jan Tumlir* made this point forcefully some 25 years ago: "The very notion of "concessions" distorts understanding by assigning positive value to protection. In this way, a mercantilist residue was preserved in the foundations of the post-World War II trade regime".[7]

Based on the mercantilist rationale, the GATT was designed as a mechanism to exchange concessions, i.e., to grant market access on a reciprocal basis. A long time before public choice theory became prominent, trade diplomats had realized that domestic public support

---

[5] For details see Patricia Schneider, *Internationale Gerichtsbarkeit als Instrument friedlicher Streitbeilegung – Von einer empirisch fundierten Theorie zu einem innovativen Konzept*, Baden-Baden 2003.

[6] Carlos M. Vazquez & John H. Jackson, *Symposium Issue on WTO Dispute Settlement Compliance: Some Reflections on Compliance with WTO Dispute Settlement Decisions*, 33 Law & Pol'y Int'l Bus. 555 *et seq.* (2002).

[7] Jan Tumlir, *International Trade Regimes and Private Property Rights*, 5 Contemporary Policy Issue 4 (April 1987).

for opening up the market for foreign competitors would only be given by ensuring increased access to foreign markets for domestic exporters in exchange. Thus, the entire rationale of an exchange of concessions has always been concerned with exporters' interests. In this regard, Art. 22 DSU is only the reverse side of an exclusively exporter-oriented perspective. Put simply, if the party to whom I have granted concessions in exchange for increased market access for my exporters fails to fulfil their legal obligation to reciprocate, I have no reason to unilaterally keep my markets open for the respective foreign exporters.

As a consequence of this, it becomes obvious that a compliance model that essentially focuses on broad public welfare considerations of world trade, such as the proposal to enable financial remedies, is not only "a useful addition to the WTO's tool box", as Marco Bronckers and Freya Baetens claim in their article in the JIEL 2013, but actually a revolutionary step. Financial remedies are 100% contrary to the rationale of WTO law. I am not saying that the current WTO rationale is convincing and should not be changed. I am simply pointing out that it is important to realize how the current system is designed.

Moreover, as indicated, in order to discuss any reform of the WTO sanctions regime, it is helpful to empirically analyze those cases in which non-compliance actually led to a suspension of concessions. In this regard, the few cases in which a suspension of concessions had been actually applied so far are more or less all characterized by a multitude of domestic and international interests involved. Those are, to name just the most important, health concerns and a special social attitude towards "unnatural" methods of food production in *EC-Hormones*, a deeply rooted special relationship with the ACP countries in *EC-Bananas*, and a 30-year-old political dispute representing almost all trade tensions that exist in US-EU relations in *US-FSC*.

I would argue that there are three important lessons to be learned from looking at the existing cases of non-compliance:

1. "[H]ard cases make bad law" (Oliver Wendell Holmes, in *Northern Securities v. US*, 1904), i.e. these cases are not suitable of serving as evidence of the functioning or non-functioning of WTO law.

2. As compliance is the rule in WTO law, it seems that the mercantilist approach of WTO law in terms of an exporter's perspective on markets entry concessions still is valid and important in political reality.

3. However, third, the few existing cases of non-compliance forcefully show the current compliance regime of WTO law does not, at least, comprehensively match with the far reaching effects of WTO law beyond market access. It is thus not possible to construe and explain WTO law exclusively from a public choice perspective of export group pressure.

However, even from an exclusive public choice perspective, it is important to realize that in order to construe a convincing non-compliance regime of WTO law, one should start off with the basic insight that non-compliance causes externalities. Thus, the question must be how to internalize the external costs of non-compliance. On the level of sanctions as a means to internalize externalities, public choice theory calls for a mechanism of internalization right at the cause of the externalities. This will not be the case if the entire WTO sanctions system is construed at an intergovernmental level, as is also the case with financial remedies, because the externalities of non-compliance with WTO occur at the level of private economic actors. Thus, an intergovernmental approach will always be only second-best. A better solution could only be realized by granting individual economic actors the right to directly rely on WTO law within the domestic legal system.

This directly leads to the necessity of a broader approach of constitutional political economy in order to convincingly analyze countermeasures in WTO law. Taking the public choice analysis into account demonstrates that a WTO sanctions regime can only be construed as a first-best solution if a public interest perspective is taken. Thus, just as with regard to national constitutions, the main question is, as *James Buchanan* phrased it, "How can Constitutions be Designed so that Politicians who Seek to Serve 'Public Interest' can Survive and Prosper".[8] This, again, necessarily requires ensuring legal rights of the individual. Moreover, it is important to think about a solution for the rent-seeking trap, i.e. the collusion between agents and special interest groups that leads to an only second-best WTO compliance regime. This requires restraints on governments, namely restraints by procedural rules. Finally, as already indicated, the most important question is how to ensure equal treatment in order to reduce incentives for rent-seeking behavior. As *Buchanan* has forcefully argued, equal treatment based on the rule of law is a central element in any system in order to ensure public interests.[9] These and other aspects that have been developed in the last years by the debate on constitutional political economy should be taken into account while discussing a possible reform of the WTO sanctions regimes in the sense of financial sanctions.

---

8   James Buchanan, *How can Constitutions be Designed so that Politicians who Seek to Serve "Public Interest" can Survive and Prosper*, 4 Constitutional Political Economy 1 (1993).
9   *Id.*

WTO Dispute Settlement and Dispute Settlement in EU FTA Agreements

Colin M. Brown[1]

Introduction

The EU has developed a consistent approach as regards dispute settlement provisions in FTAs over the last 15 years. With the increase in intensity in the EU's FTA negotiations, the standard EU approach on FTA dispute settlement will be included in a significant number of agreements. Up until now, these dispute settlement mechanisms have not been used. However, with the increase in the number of FTAs entering into application it is likely that this will not be the case much longer and that cases will be initiated in the not too distant future.

This contribution discusses the EU's FTA dispute settlement mechanisms. It does so with a particular focus on the EU-Korea FTA given that agreement is the most significant agreement currently applied, but it will be seen, for example when looking at the recently made available Singapore and other FTAs that these mechanisms are all essentially identical. The contribution will first provide an overview of the main features of the EU's standard dispute settlement mechanism. It will then focus on a comparison with the WTO DSU, focusing on the distinction between the two regimes and the inter-relationships between the two. It will, despite the fact that there have been no cases under the EU's FTAs, seek to address the question of the effectiveness of the system. It will conclude with some – by definition speculative – thoughts about how the EU's FTA standard dispute settlement mechanism may evolve over the next few years.

---

[1]   Deputy Head of Unit, Unit F2, Dispute Settlement and Legal Aspects of Trade Policy, Directorate General for Trade, European Commission and Visiting Lecturer, *Université Catholique de Louvain*. The views expressed are personal and should not be regarded as representing the view of the European Commission.

1. Main features of the EU's FTA dispute settlement mechanism

The EU has historically not engaged in FTA negotiations. These started in the early years of the 21st century with the EU's FTAs with Chile and then Mexico. However, the Global Europe strategy of 2006, adopted under the stewardship of Commissioner Mandelson saw the beginnings of a change in policy. As part of this strategy the EU started to pursue FTA negotiations with a select group of projected high-growth trading partners. The focus was put on Asia – hence the FTA with Korea and now with Singapore – and South America. However, in part in reaction to this agenda, and as part of a reaction to the 2008/2009 financial crisis and the search for new sources of growth the agenda has significantly expanded, to include Canada, Japan, and now the United States. FTAs which are currently in force which include the sophisticated FTA dispute settlement mechanism are the Russian Partnership and Co-operation Agreement, the EU-Chile FTA, the EU-Mexico FTA, the Economic Partnership Agreement between the EU and the CARIFORUM states, the EU-Korea FTA, the Euromed Agreements,[2] the EU-Central America Association Agreement,[3] the EU-Columbia/Peru/Ecuador FTA,[4] the EU-Ukraine Association Agreement,[5] the EU-Moldova Association Agreement and the EU-Georgia Association Agreement. The EU-Singapore[6] and the EU-Canada (the Comprehensive Economic and Trade Agreement) negotiations are completed and are awaiting the start of the ratification process. Negotiations including a full dispute settlement mechanism are ongoing in the following cases; EU-Vietnam, EU-Malaysia, EU-Thailand,[7] EU-Japan, EU-India,[8] EU-Malaysia, EU-US (Transatlantic Trade and investment Partnership Agreement-TTIP), EU-Mercosur, EU-China Investment Agreement, EU-Myanmar/Burma Investment Agreement, EU-Kazakhstan Partnership and Co-operation Agreement, EU-Azerbaijan Partnership and Co-operation Agreement.

These agreements go beyond traditional FTAs which focus on the reduction or elimination of substantially all tariff barriers, and include the elimination of barriers to trade in services, specific provisions tackling certain non-tariff barrier problems, detailed provisions on intellectual property and public procurement, chapters on transparency

---

[2]   E.g. Egypt, Tunisia, Morocco, Jordan.
[3]   The listed Association Agreements contain a Deep and Comprehensive FTA.
[4]   Ecuador was not an original party to this agreement, but at the time of writing – September 2014 – is expected to accede to the agreement reasonably soon.
[5]   Signature of the Ukraine agreement expected in autumn 2014.
[6]   At the time of writing – early September – some elements of the EU-Singapore FTA needed to be finalized (but unrelated to the dispute settlement mechanism.
[7]   Suspended because of the political situation in Thailand.
[8]   Suspended.

and sustainable development and investment protection (including investor-state dispute settlement), and in some cases, in particularly in the neighboring countries, the take-over of a substantial part of the EU's internal market "*acquis*". In some sectors, such as TBT or SPS the relevant WTO Agreements are incorporated into the EU Agreements. These agreements are referred to as Deep and Comprehensive Free Trade Agreements (DCFTAs).

The EU's FTA DS mechanism has the following key features:

Broadly based on the WTO DSU

In general terms the EU's DS system is based on that of the WTO. It provides for consultations, the establishment of a panel in the event that consultations do not solve the problem, a panel report, a period of time for the losing party to bring itself into conformity, the panel to rule again in the event of alleged non-compliance and ultimately the possibility of suspension of concessions.

Automaticity

The dispute settlement system is designed in such a way that the respondent cannot at any time block the progress of a particular case. As regards the selection of arbitrators, whilst there is an encouragement for an agreement on the arbitrators, either side can resort to the pre-established list of arbitrators in the event that agreement is not possible. There is no possibility for an appeal.

Selection of arbitrators

Arbitrators are selected in the first place by agreement between the parties. In the event that there is no agreement then the arbitrators are selected by lot from pre-established lists. A list is made up of equal numbers of arbitrators from the EU, from the third country concerned and of countries not party to the agreement. The latter group is tasked with acting as chairpersons. The arbitrators must meet a number of requirements both in terms of substantive knowledge and in terms of independence. The EU's agreements include a Code of Conduct for arbitrators modelled on the WTO's *Rules of conduct for the understanding on rules and procedures governing the settlement of disputes.*[9]

---

[9]   <https://www.wto.org/english/res_e/booksp_e/analytic_index_e/dsu_e.htm>.

Clarity on "sequencing"

As is well known, one of the more controversial and debated aspects of WTO dispute settlement has been the issue of "sequencing" i.e. the question of whether the successful party may, in the event of alleged non-compliance immediately move towards suspension of concessions or whether it is required that there be a compliance panel (Article 21.5 DSU). The EU's FTAs – in line with the EU's general policy – make it clear that in the event of alleged non-compliance a party needs to initiate compliance proceedings before moving to potential suspension of concessions.

Relationship to WTO Disputes

One of the criteria for the EU starting FTA negotiations is that the third country in question is a WTO Member. This creates further the possibility of disputes being taken under both the WTO and the FTA. Further, as noted above, the EU's DCFTAs often incorporate substantive WTO obligations. It has been considered necessary to seek to regulate the possibility of parallel disputes. The EU's preferred approach to this is to provide for the possibility of consecutive but not simultaneous provisions. Hence the FTAs contain a provision which prevents such simultaneous proceedings. Article 14.19 from the Korea FTA is provided below by way of example.

"Article 14.19

Relation with WTO obligations

1. Recourse to the dispute settlement provisions of this Chapter shall be without prejudice to any action in the WTO framework, including dispute settlement action.

2. However, where a Party has, with regard to a particular measure, initiated a dispute settlement proceeding, either under this Chapter or under the WTO Agreement, it may not institute a dispute settlement proceeding regarding the same measure in the other forum until the first proceeding has been concluded. In addition, a Party shall not seek redress of an obligation which is identical under this Agreement and under the WTO Agreement in the two forums. In such case, once a dispute settlement proceeding has been initiated, the Party shall not bring a claim seeking redress of the identical obligation under the other Agreement to the other forum, unless the forum selected fails for procedural or jurisdictional reasons to make findings on the claim seeking redress of that obligation.

3. For the purposes of paragraph 2:

    (a) dispute settlement proceedings under the WTO Agreement are deemed to be initiated by a Party's request for the establishment of a panel under Article 6 of the Under standing on Rules and Procedures Governing the Settlement of Disputes contained in Annex 2 of the

WTO Agreement (hereinafter referred to as the "DSU") and are deemed to be concluded when the DSB adopts the Panel's report, and the Appellate Body's report as the case may be, under Articles 16 and 17.14 of the DSU; and

(b) dispute settlement proceedings under this Chapter are deemed to be initiated by a Party's request for the establishment of an arbitration panel under Article 14.4.1 and are deemed to be concluded when the arbitration panel issues its ruling to the Parties and to the Trade Committee under Article 14.7."

Consistency with WTO interpretations

In light of the fact that the EU's DCFTAs often incorporate substantive WTO obligations a practice has developed of inserting specific guidance to panels on the interpretation of such obligations.[10] An example of that can be found in Article 14.16 of the EU-Korea FTA.

"Article 14.16

Rules of interpretation

Any arbitration panel shall interpret the provisions referred to in Article 14.2 in accordance with customary rules of interpretation of public international law, including those codified in the Vienna Convention on the Law of Treaties. Where an obligation under this Agreement is identical to an obligation under the WTO Agreement, the arbitration panel shall adopt an interpretation which is consistent with any relevant interpretation established in rulings of the WTO Dispute Settlement Body (hereinafter referred to as the "DSB"). The rulings of the arbitration panel cannot add to or diminish the rights and obligations provided for in the provisions referred to in Article 14.2."

Retaliation – link with WTO obligations

An FTA creates a separate and additional legal basis for trade relations between the two parties. For that reason it is also necessary to regulate the possibility that one or other of the Parties wishes to suspend concessions under the WTO or that one or other of the Parties wants to suspend concessions under the FTA. In the former case, it is provided that the obligations of both parties under the FTA (for example to reduce tariffs) are set aside not to prevent the suspension of concessions under the WTO.

---

[10] As an example, Article 4(1) of the EU-Korea FTA provides: "The Parties affirm their existing rights and obligations with respect to each other under the Agreement on Technical Barriers to Trade, contained in Annex 1A to the WTO Agreement (hereinafter referred to as the 'TBT Agreement') which is incorporated into and made part of this Agreement, mutatis mutandis".

In the latter case, it is provided that the WTO obligations between the parties will not prevent the suspension of concessions under the FTA. Article 14.9(4) of the EU-Korea FTA is reproduced below.

"Article 14.9

4. Nothing in this Agreement shall preclude a Party from implementing the suspension of obligations authorized by the DSB. The WTO Agreement shall not be invoked to preclude a Party from suspending obligations under this Chapter."

Mediation mechanism

A standard feature of the EU dispute settlement mechanisms is the inclusion of a mediation mechanism. This is intended to provide a forum for the amicable settlement of potential disputes. It is intended to provide another option to formal dispute settlement. Engaging in mediation is without prejudice to the possibility of formal dispute settlement.

Transparency and Amicus curiae

Another standard feature is the provision of transparency for the hearings and for the final awards. *Amicus curiae* submissions are also permitted.

Scope of coverage

The FTA DS mechanism applies to the entire FTA, unless otherwise stated. The main chapter to which it does not apply is the chapter on Sustainable Development which has a specific self-contained dispute settlement mechanism.

2. Comparison between EU FTA and WTO dispute settlement and possible inter-relationship issues

As previously noted the EU's FTA dispute settlement mechanism is largely based on the WTO DSU, with the result that many issues are tackled in a similar way. Some of the main differences and interactions of note are as follows:

Absence of a permanent secretariat

Unlike the WTO, EU FTA dispute settlement procedures do not rely on an organization to provide an institutional set-up. This implies that the choice of arbitrators on which there is not agreement does not fall to an institutional figure, such as the Director General of the WTO, but rather is managed through a blind choice from the pre-agreed list of arbitrators by the chair of the relevant institutional body. It means also that the arbitrators cannot rely on the support of an organization for either management of the case or for assistance on substantive matters. For that reason, one of the elements foreseen is the possibility for the arbitrators to use assistants.

Absence of an appellate mechanism

Unlike for the WTO there is no appellate mechanism foreseen. The absence of such a mechanism is in recognition that creating a mechanism which would cover all of the EU's different agreements with different partners is a virtually impossible task and that the expected frequency of disputes is such that the costs of setting up and maintaining an appellate mechanism on a bilateral basis is in most cases too significant as compared to the expected benefits.

Relationship between FTA and WTO dispute settlement

The expectation is that, since the EU's FTAs are with other WTO members, either party would, in the event of a dispute consider carefully whether to use either the WTO or the FTA dispute settlement mechanism. Evidently some disputes will only be possible under the FTA dispute settlement mechanism where the dispute concerns the implementation of an FTA specific obligation. Equally, in some cases a dispute would only be possible under the WTO dispute settlement mechanism.

The incorporation of WTO obligations into the FTA has a dispute settlement related objective. It is to permit litigation where it is suspected that the party concerned is breaching both the substantive WTO obligations and some of the so-called WTO plus obligations in the FTA. This has the significant advantage of permitting one case under the FTA to bring about compliance with all of the obligations which the third country in question owes to the EU (and vice-versa of course). It might be that that advantage would be outweighed in specific cases by the advantages which would arise in the WTO in terms either of acting with co-complainants or in terms of the systemic value of a ruling by the WTO Appellate Body. That would inevitably be a case-by-case judgment. Nevertheless, the principle of *res judicata* applies where an identical obligation would be subject to litigation both in the FTA and the WTO.

Such an approach does not, it is suggested, appear to raise any specific problems as regards the WTO. Given that the substantive WTO obligations are incorporated into the FTA as any other obligations they are being litigated in the FTA context as specific FTA obligations rather than as WTO obligations *per se*. The results of such litigation are not binding on any WTO panel examining the same issue, but they may be considered useful and even persuasive. As previously noted the FTA panel will be obliged to follow any interpretation developed by a WTO panel or the WTO Appellate Body.

Transparency and Amicus curiae

As is well known, open hearings have been held in the WTO and *amicus curiae* submissions have been held by the Appellate Body to be permissible. Nevertheless open hearings have taken place only where the disputing parties have agreed and hence there are still numerous cases where the hearings have not been open to the public. Similarly, whilst the Appellate Body has ruled in favor of permitting *amicus curiae* submissions this reading of the WTO DSU has not found unanimous support amongst WTO Members. This contrasts with the EU's FTA practice, which has clearly established the desirability of open hearings and permitting *amicus curiae* submissions.

3. Effectiveness of the different mechanisms

It is not possible to reach a conclusion on the effectiveness of the EU's FTA system at this moment in time given the first cases have not yet occurred. It is assumed that, with the intensification first of negotiations and then of agreements entering into force there will be a significant number of such bilateral cases in the future.

The effectiveness of the WTO dispute settlement mechanism is well-established. It remains to be seen how the size of the parties to the FTAs affects the use of bilateral FTAs. Evidently, the EU is one of the main users of the WTO DSU, and its approach to dispute settlement as less of a political act than a sign of a normal way of doing business between sophisticated economies is often at odds with the views of other actors. Moreover, the relative weight of retaliation from an economy the size of the EU would be a factor which might play out differently in FTA dispute settlement as compared to WTO dispute settlement.

4. Possible improvements to FTA dispute settlement

Given there have not yet been cases under the EU's FTA dispute settlement mechanism it is difficult to make specific predictions about possible improvements. However, at least two possible sources of inspiration can be identified.

First, as is well known, the EU is now negotiating agreements including investor-state dispute settlement. The standard system of investor-state dispute settlement (ISDS) has a number of features which are set up in a different manner from those of the WTO DSU from which the EU's FTA dispute settlement system is derived. It may be that some features from ISDS practice have an influence on the EU's FTA dispute settlement practice. One example is the conclusion of new rules on transparency for ISDS in the context of the United Nations Commission for International Trade Law (UNCITRAL). These rules are the first agreed rules on transparency in international economic law and have a number of features which are different from standard FTA practice. One such feature is the requirement that the submissions and other documents made by the disputing parties should be made public.

Second, the EU has started developing specific dispute settlement mechanisms for specific issues. One such mechanism is the emergency procedures for the settlement of energy disputes which are included in the Ukraine, Georgia and Moldova Association Agreements. These form an integral part of the standard FTA dispute settlement mechanism and essentially consist in shortened time periods and a specific approach to remedies. It remains to be seen whether this practice of developing a specific approach for certain types of disputes has an influence on the overall FTA dispute settlement practice.

***

A Comment

Pieter Jan KUIJPER[1]

Colin Brown's paper has described to us the very comprehensive dispute settlement system for trade disputes that will be introduced with the CETA. This regional dispute settlement system raises two systemic questions. First, what is the relation with the WTO and its dispute settlement system and, more particularly is it a hierarchical relationship? Secondly what is the relationship with the ISDS system in the same treaty and more particularly how to distinguish clearly between trade rights and investment rights?

To begin with the first question, there is no doubt that FTA's like the one between the EU and Canada need to be in conformity with the requirements of Article XXIV GATT and Article V GATS, but there seem to be sufficient reasons for assuming that this is the case. On the other hand there is still some doubt how far the powers of the parties to an FTA go, when contracting out of the WTO Agreements, as long as the requirements of those articles have been fulfilled. In other words, does the hierarchy between WTO and FTA's as created by Article XXIV and V go further than the terms of those articles? The Appellate Body reports in *Turkey – Textiles (DS 34)* and in *Peru – Agricultural Products (DS 457)* seem to answer this question in the affirmative. Especially the latter case, concerning the FTA between Peru and Guatemala, the AB does so because the Peruvian system akin to a price-band system is contrary to Article 4(2) of the Agreement on Agriculture and not because this system breaches the norm of the coverage of "substantially all the trade" by the FTA (which would have required the AB to look into the question whether the Peruvian system had such serious consequences for agricultural trade between the FTA partners as to amount to a breach of this threshold for establishing a proper FTA).[2] In this way the AB has extended the hierarchy between the WTO Agreements and FTA's beyond the term of Articles XXIV and V, thus impeding the application of the normal rules of the law of treaties on the relationship between multilateral treaties and bilateral agreements between two parties modifying the

---

[1] Professor, Law School, University of Amsterdam.
[2] The AB does not make clear, as the Panel did, that the FTA had not actually entered into force and that, therefore, it was not necessary to look at the case from that perspective.

multilateral treaty *inter se*. Whether this was indeed the AB's intention or not, needs to be cleared up by the AB itself in a later case or by the Member States through an interpretative declaration under Article IX:2 of the WTO Agreement.

As to the second question, it is basically about how to avoid overlap between the two dispute settlement systems in the CETA. How to avoid making the co-existence between the two procedures inadvertently into a paradise for lawyers? In my view the agreement does a great deal to prevent this from happening. There may be one situation, however, where this may be virtually impossible, namely the cases in which a right under the trade part of the agreement is identical to a right under the investment part. This is the case with the intellectual property rights under TRIPs, which in many BITs and also in the investment part of the CETA, are described as property rights that qualify as investments. Perhaps there is still work to do here, not just in CETA, but also in other situations where investment and trade agreements are included in one instrument or in parallel treaties between the same parties.

Going on from these rather fundamental questions, I would like to turn to two more practical problems where the co-existence of FTA courts with the WTO dispute settlement system is concerned. The first one relates to the composition of the FTA court and the second one to the so-called fork-in-the-road and no-turning-back provisions.

On the first question, it is impossible to overstate the importance of making the selection procedure for panels of the FTA dispute settlement system absolutely watertight. There is a lesson to learn here from the Mexico-US conflict on HFCS, which started with a procedure in the NAFTA system, in which the provision on panel composition, which seemed watertight, was nevertheless subverted by the US. The US simply "forgot" to submit its list of trade law experts from which the US Members of panels could be picked. When thereupon Mexico unilaterally took countermeasures against the US, the latter activated the WTO dispute settlement system arguing that these countermeasures were contrary to Article III GATT and won the resulting case hands down (*Mexico – Soft Drinks, DS 304*). Even after ten years I remain of the view that this constituted an egregious abuse of the WTO dispute settlement system with a view to "remedying" the malfunction of a regional dispute settlement system – a task the WTO dispute settlement system should never have adopted. The EU should do everything to avoid a repeat performance of this tragedy.

The best way to do so may be to go back to one of the classical ways in which to compose inter-State arbitral tribunals. The complaining party begins by choosing "its arbitrator", and if the defendant party refuses to appoint its arbitrator in its turn, the arbitrator of the complaining party becomes the sole arbitrator. Combined with the well-known mechanism to have the presiding arbitrator appointed by a neutral authority, this is a fool-proof way of having a panel appointed with the least amount of fuss.[3]

The second practical problem I wanted to deal with is the relation between the jurisdiction of the panels (and, in future, perhaps also appeal courts) in FTA dispute settlement systems and the jurisdiction of the panels and the Appellate Body of the WTO in the light of the fork-in-the-road and no-turning-back provisions ruling the choice of which dispute settlement to use in case of a dispute. These provisions in CETA in principle are well drafted and do indeed guarantee that once a trajectory for a dispute is chosen, it must be finished. Once that trajectory is finished and a final ruling obtained either within the FTA dispute settlement system or the WTO system, however, does "no turning back" include a resort to the other system as well? In my view it should, but I am not 100% sure that it does. But that may matter little because of the jurisdiction of both systems.

The FTA dispute settlement has competence to decide disputes under the FTA and not under the WTO, but the FTA includes provisions that are (near)-identical to WTO provisions. These can be applied and interpreted by the WTO dispute settlement system, not as FTA norms, but as WTO norms. The WTO dispute settlement system, on the other hand, has no jurisdiction on the basis of the DSU to rule on disputes containing FTA norms, whether they are pure FTA norms or WTO plus norms. Assuming that most disputes would contain a mix of claims based on (near)-identical WTO norms, WTO plus norms and specific FTA norms, there would hardly be a dispute that could fruitfully be submitted to a WTO panel. Only an isolated dispute about a pure WTO norm in an FTA could be usefully brought directly to WTO dispute settlement, but then only as a dispute about a WTO norm. Only if an FTA Disputes panel were to rule in such a dispute contrary to established Appellate Body case-law (which the CETA text encourages it to follow), it may be useful to restart a procedure on the same issue before the WTO dispute settlement organs. However, it may be more fruitful to start thinking, and perhaps even negotiating in the WTO, about a preliminary reference procedure from FTA panels to the WTO dispute settlement system with a view of maintaining a minimum coherence in international trade law. It may sound far-fetched, but so was a binding dispute settlement in the WTO itself before the negotiations were started.

---

[3] It may even be worthwhile to consider this system for WTO panel composition, if an amendment of the DSU were found to be feasible. A system as the present one, in which the DG must intervene in the composition of panels in 75% of the cases, is clearly malfunctioning.

Five Scenarios in Search of a Director

WTO Judges, Their Terms of References, Scope of Competence, Remedies they Proscribe, and the Consequences for the Addressees

Louise JOHANNESSON[1] & Petros C. MAVROIDIS[2]

Abstract

The WTO has been lauded for its unique dispute settlement system. Its uniqueness lies primarily in that it is the most comprehensive "compulsory third party" adjudication regime in international relations. No other regime of this breadth exists in state to state relations. Without assigning a cause to effect relationship, we point to factors that might be further researched in order to show to what extent they constitute prerequisites for emulating compulsory third party adjudication. Pragmatic judgments constitute a factor to be reckoned with. WTO judges are typically "Geneva crowd", and they feel comfortable with judgments that do not prejudge too much national sovereignty. The institution is further happy to talk compliance up, using proxies rather than accurate information to this effect.

1. Introductory Remarks

In his monumental study of 1993, Hudec made a very persuasive claim to the effect that the WTO dispute settlement system did not transition to compulsory third party adjudication overnight. The GATT started as a "relational contract" among few, like-minded players. Years of pragmatic judgments that followed, developed a trade ethos of respecting the agreed deeds, while deviations would be tolerated in the short run. *De facto* endorsing prospective remedies, by not objecting to dozens of recommendations by Panels to this effect, was one more step in this direction.

---

[1]   Örebro University, and IFN (Institute of Industrial Economics), Stockholm;
[2]   Edwin B. Parker Professor of Law at Columbia Law School (on leave at EUI). We would like to thank Julie Pain, and Rhian-Mary Wood-Richards for graciously spending time answering to our many questions.

In this paper, we look into five issues that largely reflect the "pragmatic" nature of the GATT. We do not purport to argue that it is because of these factors, that the WTO has moved to compulsory third party adjudication, and indeed we personally do not agree wholeheartedly with the emerging picture. We do believe nevertheless, that facts reveal a story, which might surprise the un-initiated in similar research.

In short, it is not all so rosy as it is often portrayed, and some issues are indeed worth thinking about and even amending in the future. The purpose of this paper is not to propose reforms. It is to provide an adequate description of reality. The paper is structured as follows. In Section 2, we discuss the identity and function of WTO "judges", and in Section 3 the clerks aiding them. In Section 4 we move to discuss the law WTO judges use, and in Section 5 the remedies they propose to undo the effects of illegalities. In Section 6, we move to discuss compliance at the WTO level, the end game of remedies suggested by judges aided by their clerks. Section 7 concludes.

2. Appointing Judges at the WTO

2.1 Panelists

2.1.1 Nomination

According to the DSU:

(a) three Panelists will serve a Panel, unless parties agree to a Panel consisting of five Panelists (Art. 8.5);

(b) it is the WTO Secretariat that has the initiative to propose Panelists (8.6);

(c) it can propose Panelists from the indicative list ("roster") of Panelists which is kept at the WTO. It is WTO Members that can propose individuals for inclusion in the list, which divides the roster Panelists into "governmental" and non-governmental (8.4);

(d) if the parties agree with the Panelists proposed by the Secretariat, then the Panel will be established. Agreement of the parties is the sufficient condition to this effect. Nevertheless, if they disagree with respect to one or more Panelists proposed, then the complainant or the defendant can request from the Director-General (DG) of the WTO to establish or complete the Panel (8.7). Disagreements with proposed names must be based on "compelling reasons"(8.6);

(e) the right to request the DG to establish/complete the Panel cannot be exercised before 20 days from the establishment of the Panel have lapsed, e.g. 20 days from the date when the Dispute Settlement

Body (DSB) has agreed to establish a Panel to adjudicate a particular dispute (8.7);

(f) the DG has discretion to establish the Panel. He must consult with the Chairmen of the DSB and the competent committee, but does not have to follow their advice (8.7).

In practice, all Panels established in the WTO-era so far have been composed of three Panelists. A nomination for inclusion in the roster has never been turned down so far.

The parties can reject the nomination of Panelists only for "compelling reasons". Practice, which we visit *infra*, suggests that requests to the DG to "complete" the Panel happen very frequently. This should mean that either "compelling reasons" arise too often (and then maybe the legislator had underestimated the frequency of occurrence), or that this term has been interpreted in rather relaxed manner. It is very difficult any further in this area, which belongs to the sphere of private information: proposals for Panelists take place behind closed doors. One thing is for sure: nationality emerges as one "compelling reason". There is only one case, US-Zeroing (EC), where nationals of a litigating party served in a Panel. In this case, Bill Davey, a US national, and Hans Beseler, a German national, served together as Panelists in a dispute between the EU and the US.[3]

The DG customarily meets not only with the two Chairmen (Dispute Settlement Body, General Council), but also with the members of the WTO Legal Service, and/or Services or Rules Division (if the case concerns trade in services, or contingent protection) when establishing the Panel.

2.1.2 Who Gets the Nod?

Here we should explain our panelist classification. The first, general division is whether panelists' main employer is governmental or non-governmental. We further subdivide non-governmental into academic or private practice-. Finally, we check whether the panelists were or have been a Geneva resident (a longer stay) at the time of their appointment, for both categories.

During the period 1995–2014, 245 panelists have served on 224 panels. This means that we have a dispute-panelist dyad (or "panel appointments") of 672. First, only 30% of all panelists have been chosen from the indicative list.[4]

---

[3] This happens routinely though before the AB. In the GATT years, nationals did serve on occasion on Panels. Bob Hudec for example, a US citizen, served as Panelist in US-Customs User Fee; Andy Lowenfeld (US), and Pierre Pescatore (Luxembourg) served as Panelists in US-Section 337, a dispute between the EU and the US.

[4] 77 panelists were not on the indicative list at the time of appointment, but were added on the list afterwards.

Around 60% of those have been employed by the government at the time of appointment.[5] Non-governmental panelists comprise of 25% private sector employees, mostly private consultants or lawyers in private practices. The smallest group is panelists employed as academic with 13%. But in this group 58% have formerly been employed by the government,[6] so that 74% of all panel appointments include government of former government officials.

Prior to the first panel appointment for a panelist, 66–76% had previously been in contact with WTO in some capacity and/or is a current resident of Geneva. This includes panelists that took part in GATT and its negotiations. We give a range for this statistic since it unfortunately is a little more unreliable than employment at the time of appointment.[7]

Even though we have 33% missing data, we can give a hint of their educational background, since we see no reasons why it wouldn't be representative. 40% of all panels have had panelists with a legal background, with various level of degree. Whereas 16% have an economics background and 12% have stated other degrees.

2.1.3 Remuneration

The DSU does not say much about remuneration of Panelists, other than (8.11):

> Panelists' expenses, including travel and subsistence allowance, shall be met from the WTO budget in accordance with criteria to be adopted by the General Council, based on recommendations of the Committee on Budget, Finance and Administration.

In practice, following an unofficial "memorandum" dating from 1992, the following applies:

(a) governmental Panelists do not get reimbursed for Panel work. They will get reimbursed for travelling, if they are not Geneva-based;

(b) non-governmental Panelists will get reimbursed 600 CHF/day of work. They will also receive a 437 CHF/day per diem to cover expenses incurred when participating in Panel hearings in Geneva. Finally, they can request money for work done in preparation of meetings. In the overwhelming majority of cases,

---

[5]   1.6% (11 dispute-panelists) is missing.

[6]   7% (17 dispute-panelists) are missing.

[7]   Unless they clearly state in their curricula vitae, official biographies or if they have or had employment as a WTO delegate or similar it can't be conclusively determined what kind contact they have had with Geneva in general, WTO in particular. Undetermined are around 12% (78 panel appointments) for this variable.

they do not request honoraria for more than 10 days per dispute, paid at 600 CHF/day.

The WTO is non-transparent in this respect, and the information we have included here is based on interviews with former Panelists.

2.1.4 Function

Panels have standard reference, unless if agreed otherwise by the parties to a dispute, namely (Art. 7 DSU):

> To examine, in the light of the relevant provisions in (name of the covered agreement(s) cited by the parties to the dispute), the matter referred to the DSB by (name of party) in document […] and to make such findings as will assist the DSB in making the recommendations or in giving the rulings provided for in that/those agreement(s).

This is hardly a self-interpreting statement, and it says nothing about sources of law they can use, standard of review etc. One thing is clear: Panelists are "agents" with a limited mandate; they are not "principals". They must ensure the "policy space" committed to the WTO by the "principals", the WTO Members. Art. 3.2 DSU reads to this effect:

> Recommendations and rulings of the DSB cannot add to or diminish the rights and obligations provided in the covered agreements.

To this effect, they will issue "recommendations" when a violation has been established, and may issue "suggestions" as well (Art. 19 DSU). The former have standardized content, namely (Art. 19.1 DSU):

> that the Member concerned bring the measure into conformity with that agreement.

Suggestions do what their name indicates: they "suggest" specific ways to achieve compliance, e.g. to bring measures into conformity with the WTO. They are optional, and non-binding. Although transaction costs could be heavily reduced if followed, WTO Members can lawfully disregard them. Practice evidences that they have been followed a few times only so far.[8] We will return to this point, and discuss it in more detail *infra*.

---

[8] Mavroidis and Wu (2012) include a list of suggestions issued between 1995 and 2012.

2.2 ABMs (Appellate Body Members)

2.2.1 Nomination

A Preparatory Committee was established (where delegates at the DSB could participate) in order to decide on the selection process for the members of the AB. Following a recommendation by this body, the DSB decided that an organ be established comprising the DG of the WTO, and the Chairmen of the General Council, the DSB, the CTG (Council for Trade in Goods), the CTS (Council for Trade in Services), and the TRIPs (Trade-related Intellectual Property Rights) Council. This organ would be receiving propositions for nominations by WTO Members, and, at the end, propose to the DSB its nominees. It is the DSB that would appoint the members of the AB.[9] Individuals are nominated for a four year term, which is renewable once.

Art. 17.1 DSU states that three rotating members of the AB (a division) will hear a case. The formula for selection of a division is not reflected in the DSU or in the AB WP (Working Procedures), and is unknown to the wider public (Rule 6 WP).[10] A presiding member for each division will be selected (Rule 7 WP). Although a division hears and decides a particular case (Rule 3 WP), a practice of collegiality has developed. In an effort to promote consistency and coherence in decision-making, Rule 4 WP reflects the so-called collegiality-requirement: according to its § 3, the members of a division will exchange views with members of the AB who do not participate in their division, on the resolution of the dispute before them. The final decision of course will be taken by the members of the division alone.

---

[9] WTO Doc. WT/DSB/1 of June 19, 1995.

[10] Anecdotally, it seems that on its appointment, each member of the AB receives a number. A combination of three numbers, rotating according to a *secret formula*, will hear appeals as they are coming to the AB. For example, numbers 1, 2 and 5 will hear appeal against DS 1, numbers 2, 6 and 9 will hear appeals against DS2 and so on. What is unknown is the *formula* for rotating the divisions.

2.2.2 Who Gets the Nod?

The following table lists those who have been proposed so far

Name	#Disputes	Nationality	Term of Office	Property	Former Panelist	Panelist after AB
Abi-Saab	28	Egypt	2000–2008	A		
Bacchus	34	US	1995–2003	FG/P		
Baptista	17	Brazil	2001–2009	P		Yes
Bautista	8	Philippines	2007–2011	FG	Yes	
Beeby	12	New Zealand	1995–2000	FG		
Ehlermann	27	EU	1995–2001	FG		
El-Naggar	14	Egypt	1995–2000	A/P		
Feliciano	25	Philippines	1995–2001	A/FG		
Ganesan	25	India	2000–2008	FG	Yes	
Hillman	13	US	2007–2011	FG		
Janow	9	US	2003–2007	A/FG	Yes	
Lacarte-Muró	27	Uruguay	1995–2001	FG	Yes	Yes
Lockhart	19	Australia	2001–2006	FG/P		
Matsushita	16	Japan	1995–2000	A		
Oshima	8	Japan	2008–2012	FG		
Sacerdoti	24	EU	2001–2009	A		
Taniguchi	20	Japan	2000–2007	A		
Unterhalter	10	South Africa	2006–2013	P	Yes	
Graham*	4	US	2011–	FG/P		
Ramírez-Hernández*	20	Mexico	2009–	FG		
Chang*	7	Korea	2012–	A		
Bhatia*	11	India	2011–	FG		
Van den Bossche*	11	EU	2009–	A		
Zhang*	16	China	2008–	FG	Yes	
Servansing*	0	Mauritius	2014-	FG		

Complete list of former and current AB Members up until February 2015

A few observations seem warranted:

(a) the preference for former government officials (over 60% of all appointments) is clear and it cuts across trading partners, in the sense that all of them share this preference;

(b) practitioners and academics are more or less of equal number, and definitely a minority across all appointments;

(c) fourteen WTO Members have shared all AB members. EU, Japan, and the US have appointed three each; Egypt, India, and Philippines, two each; Australia, Brazil, China, Korea, Mexico, New Zealand, South Africa, and Uruguay have appointed one member each;

(d) there has never been an AB term without an EU or US member.

First, around 64% of all current and former AB Members have been former government officials. And they have adjudicated around 65% of all disputes that transitioned into appeals. Second, fourteen WTO Members have shared all AB members. EU, Japan, and the US have appointed three each; Egypt, India, and Philippines, two each; Australia, Brazil, China, Korea, Mexico, New Zealand, South Africa, and Uruguay have appointed one member each. And lastly, there has never been an AB term without an EU or US member.

A typical AB Member is male, with a tenure of around 75 months (6 years) with 16 disputes during that time. He or she is most likely a former government official that is 60 years old at the start of the term of office.

Figure 1: Average number of disputes adjudicated by AB Member.

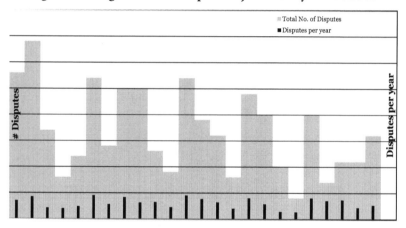

*Current Appellate Body Member (February, 2015)

2.2.3 Remuneration

The lack of transparency that we observed with respect to the remuneration of Panelists is evident here as well. WT/DSB/1, the Decision Establishing the AB cited *supra*, reads in §12:

> The amount of a retainer/fee package would have to be large enough to offset a member's opportunity cost of work foregone because of potential conflicts of interest, or incompatibility with sporadic trips to Geneva. [...] the compensation should be high enough to provide an incentive for a member not to take on work which might create a conflict of interest. Accordingly, it would appear that the retainer should be set at a minimum of SF 7,000 per month, plus a fully-adequate daily fee, travel expenses and a per diem. The actual amounts should be set on the basis of further research on current rates for equivalent services under similar conditions.

The wording might suggest that members of the AB will be paid asymmetrically, since the opportunity cost cannot be the same say for a practicing attorney in a leading law firm, and a mid-level bureaucrat. In practice though, they are paid the same amount for work done. Work done however, can be asymmetric for two reasons:

(a) the formula for appointment in a Division is unknown. Empirically, however, we know that some AB members have been appointed more often than others, as our Table xx shows;

(b) besides the 7,000 Swiss francs per month (which have been adjusted since 1995), AB members can request compensation for work done at home on any given case. The compensation is fixed at around 780 CHF/day of work. The amount of compensation requested depends on various factors ranging from the complexity of the case to the personal ethics of individuals involved.

It seems that they are paid on yearly basis more than the stated *supra statutory sum*, but it is highly unclear (because of lack of transparency) who gets paid what.[11]

2.2.4 Function

The AB decides in last resort. It hears appeals against Panel reports (Art. 17.1 DSU), can uphold, modify or reject appealed Panel findings (Art. 17.13 DSU), and, in doing that, must be limited to issues of law (Art. 17.6 DSU). Panels are the trier of facts, the AB cannot revisit facts in order to re-establish de novo the factual record.

Since its review is based on issues of law, almost by construction, its function is to provide interpretations of the provisions that could, in principle, apply across cases. There is nothing binding *stare decisis* in the WTO legal system. De facto nevertheless, the system comes close to that. In US – Stainless Steel (Mexico), the AB re-visited all prior case law, and held that it expected Panels to follow prior AB findings dealing with the same issue (§158):

> It is well settled that Appellate Body reports are not binding, except with respect to resolving the particular dispute between the parties. This, however, does not mean that subsequent panels are free to disregard the legal interpretations and the *ratio decidendi* contained in previous Appellate Body reports that have been adopted by the DSB. In *Japan – Alcoholic Beverages II*, the Appellate Body found that:

---

[11] WTO Doc. WT/DFA/W/115 mentions in p. 88 that AB expenditure for that year was 624,000 Swiss francs. This sum exceeds the statutory amount by at least 40,000 Swiss francs. Take into account that this was the budget for 2005. The budgetary prediction for 2015 is 2,000,000 Swiss francs that have been committed to the AB.

[a]dopted panel reports are an important part of the GATT *acquis*. They are often considered by subsequent panels. They create legitimate expectations among WTO Members, and, therefore, should be taken into account where they are relevant to any dispute. (Italics in the original)

In US – Shrimp (Article 21.5 – Malaysia), the AB clarified that this reasoning applies to adopted AB reports as well.

3. Support Mechanism: WTO Clerks

3.1 Panel-Stage

Art. 27.1 DSU reads:

The Secretariat shall have the responsibility of assisting panels, especially on the legal, historical and procedural aspects of the matters dealt with, and of providing secretarial and technical support.

Panels are aided by law clerks. Contrary to the US tradition, clerks are not assigned to individual judges, but to the Panel as such. Law clerks have to pass a competition to this effect, and join the WTO. That is, law clerks' allegiance is to the WTO, its case law so far etc., and not to particular justices as is the case for example, of clerks to the US Supreme Court.

Practice suggests that, depending on the subject-matter and administrative capacity, different divisions will assist Panels. Typically, a Legal Officer and a Secretary assist Panels. The Legal Officer will be a member of the WTO Legal Affairs Division, unless if the dispute concerns a contingent protection instrument. In this case, the Legal Affairs Officer will be a member of the WTO Rules Division. A similar arrangement is in place whenever litigation focuses on trade in services, and in this case a member of the WTO GATS Division will act as Legal Officer.

Secretaries are chosen from the *ratione materiae* competent Division, e.g. a member of the WTO Agriculture Division will act as Secretary in cases involving interpretation of the WTO Agreement on Agriculture.

3.2 AB-Stage

The AB as well, has its own Legal Service. The conditions for recruitment are identical to those for the WTO Secretariat.

3.3 Clerks or Quasi Judges?

Panel deliberations are confidential (Art. 14.1 DSU). The proceedings of the AB are confidential as well (Art. 17.10 DSU). As a result, it is difficult to assess what happens behind closed doors. What we care about in this paper is whether clerks behave as such or, conversely, whether they are more influential than clerks typically are.

Nordstrom (2005) hints that this is the case indeed, although recognizes the limits of the factual record he has established. There are good reasons to believe that Nordstrom's analysis comes close to the truth.

First, as stated above, WTO Panelists are either unpaid for the service they provide, or paid a honorarium (600 CHF/day). The majority of Panelists are government officials, who do the work for free. The WTO has not put in place monetary incentives for Panelists, that much is for sure.

Second, think in terms of the opportunity cost. Government officials give up on their government work in order to resolve disputes. It is of course easier for large delegations to "take one for the team" and distribute the work of the missing delegate between them. It is more difficult for smaller delegations. Horn *et al.* (2011) provide the numbers showing that delegates from EU, US (the large delegations) become Panelists in about 10% of the time. Delegates from smaller delegations will thus, have even less of an incentive to work as Panelists.

Why not refuse then? Probably, they do not refuse, because the appointment as Panelist is good for their career development. The best of both worlds for them is to accept nominations while "outsourcing" the work associated with the nomination.

Third, there is an issue of expertise involved. WTO law has become quite voluminous, since the WTO became the busiest state to state court around. Knowledge of past case law is imperative in a system of law that prides in being "consistent". Consistency (assuming one is not consistently correct) is incentive compatible structure for any adjudicating forum, since this is the best proxy for "independence" and "impartiality".

For consistency to be thus served, expertise is necessary input. Expertise nevertheless, should not be taken for granted, and it is likelier that it resides with members of the WTO Secretariat than with "amateur" judges.

Taking all this on board would suggest that the interests of amateur judges are best served when:

(a) They can pride that they have served as Panelists;

(b) Panel time has not been too much of distraction from their day to day occupation;

(c) They have "outsourced" the work associated with the preparation of the "issues paper" that serves as basis for Panel deliberations, the drafting of award, the consistency of the award with prior rulings on the same issue to those with the expertise to do a good job, e.g. the members of the WTO Secretariat.

The situation is probably a bit different with respect to members of the AB. Much of our discussion *supra* nevertheless, finds application there as well. All this to suggest that, while the Secretariat has no authority to interpret the various provisions in the WTO Agreement and should serve rather than lead the Panel, there are good arguments that the line between "serve" and "lead" is more of a line in the sand rather than set in stone.

4. Terms of Reference

4.1 Panels

Panels have standards terms of reference, unless if parties to a dispute agree to special terms (Art. 7 DSU). Special terms were sparingly agreed only in the WTO era (see for example, US-Gasoline; Brazil-Desiccated Coconut).

The key issue regarding terms of reference has to do with the question whether Panels (and the AB) will use WTO law only to resolve disputes before them, or conversely, whether they will "outsource" law. In Mavroidis (2008), following comprehensive analysis of the facts, the conclusion was that Panels only sparingly will use non-WTO law, and they will do so, as supplementary means of interpretation.

This cautious attitude has been widely applauded by the Membership, and has some rational basis as well.[12]

4.2 AB

There is no corresponding to Art. 7 DSU provision that concerns the AB. Its terms of reference for the AB are circumscribed by the appeals before it. Our discussion above regarding sources of law is relevant here as well.

5. Recommendations and Suggestions (Policy Space)

A ruling, that is, a finding of inconsistency is the necessary condition for Panels to recommend that the WTO Member concerned brings its

---

[12] In Horn and Mavroidis (2014), we advanced the argument that this attitude guarantees that the same law will apply to the whole Membership across disputes.

measures into compliance with the WTO. Panels may also suggest ways to do so.[13] Art. 19.1 DSU reads:

> Where a panel or the AB concludes that a measure is inconsistent with a covered agreement, it shall recommend that the Member concerned bring the measure into conformity with that agreement. In addition to its recommendations, the panel or AB may suggest ways in which the Member concerned could implement the recommendations.

5.1 Recommendations

WTO Panels, except for extreme cases developed in case law, must issue a recommendation every time the complainant has successfully met its burden of proof.[14]

Art. 19 DSU leaves WTO adjudicating bodies no discretion as to the substantive content of a recommendation: the author of the illegal act must bring its measures into compliance.[15]

As a result, a recommendation leaves its addressees with substantial discretion as to what needs to be done for compliance to be achieved.[16] The need for discretion when it comes to implementing a report by a WTO adjudicating body has been best described in the panel report in *US – Section 301 Trade Act*:

---

[13] There is of course no need for a ruling of inconsistency in case an NVC (non-violation complaint), or in case of a "situation complaint". In similar cases a recommendation (and/or suggestion) will be issued any time the conditions for the successful invocation of the two types of complaints have been met. The AB as well can recommend and/or suggest under the same conditions as Panels.

[14] A recommendation is not necessary in case the challenged measure is no longer in place. To this effect, in *US – Certain EC Products*, the AB ruled that (§ 81): "The Panel erred in recommending that the DSB request the United States to bring into conformity with its WTO obligations a measure which the Panel has found no longer exists." Subsequent Panels (*India – Autos* §§ 8.14ff.) have confirmed this view. In *US – Large Civil Aircraft (2nd Complaint)*, the Panel refused to issue a recommendation (although it had established the inconsistency of the challenged measure with the WTO) because the recommendation issued at the first complaint was still operative, § 8.6.

[15] See, for example, § 7.24 of the Panel report in *EC – Commercial Vessels*, where the Panel rejected a request by Korea to recommend "that the European Communities immediately cease any further disbursements of illegal funding". In its view, the only recommendation it could make is (eventually) that the defendant bring its measures into compliance with its obligations. There is one exception so far: in *US – Suspended Concession*, the AB recommended "that the Dispute settlement Body request the United states and the European Communities to initiate Article 21.5 proceedings without delay in order to resolve their disagreement as to whether the European Communities has removed the measure found to be inconsistent in *EC – Hormones* and whether the application of the suspension of concessions by the United States remains legally valid." (§ 737).

[16] The WTO Member concerned cannot of course continue and/or repeat the same behavior.

The obligation on Members to bring their laws into conformity with WTO obligations is a fundamental feature of the system and, despite the fact that it affects the internal legal system of a State, has to be applied rigorously. At the same time, enforcement of this obligation must be done in the least intrusive way possible. The Member concerned must be allowed the maximum autonomy in ensuring such conformity and, if there is more than one lawful way to achieve this, should have the freedom to choose that way which suits it best (§ 7.102).

A recommendation will be part of a DSB decision addressed to the WTO Member concerned, and is binding upon its addressee.

5.2 Suggestions

Through a suggestion, Panels will suggest ways to implement an adverse finding. Art. 19 DSU states that suggestions are meant to facilitate the implementation of recommendations.

A complaining party may request a suggestion, but Panels do not have to grant them. The Panel in *US – Stainless Steel (Mexico)* refused to issue a suggestion, because it had previously refused to issue a recommendation, since the challenged measure had already expired (§ 8.5). In *US – Lead and Bismuth II* the Panel faced a request by the EU:

> to suggest that the United States amend its countervailing duty laws to recognize the principle that a privatization at market prices extinguishes subsidies. (§ 8.2).

Since however, the EU had not identified the specific provision of US law, the Panel declined to make a suggestion to the effect requested. In *US – Stainless Steel*, Korea requested the Panel to suggest that the US revoke the anti-dumping order in place. The Panel refused to accept Korea's claim, stating:

> Article 19.1 of the DSU allows but does not require a panel to make a suggestion where it deems it appropriate to do so. (§ 7.8)

The Panel however added that, in its view, revocation of the antidumping order would be one way for the US to bring their measures into compliance but not the only way to do so (§ 7.10). In *EC – Pipe Fittings*, the Panel held that (§ 8.11):

> By virtue of Article 19.1 of the *DSU*, a panel has discretion to ("may") suggest ways in which a Member could implement the recommendation that the Member concerned bring the measure into conformity with the covered agreement in question. Clearly, however, a panel is by no means required to make a suggestion should it not deem it appropriate to do so. Thus, while we are free to suggest ways in which we believe the European Communities

could appropriately implement our recommendation, we decide not to do so in this case.[17]

In *Guatemala – Cement I*, Mexico, requested the Panel to recommend that Guatemala revoke the measure and also "refund those anti-dumping duties already collected" (§ 8.1). The Panel declined, noting that Art. 19.1 DSU requests from Panels to recommend that the Member bring its measures into conformity (§ 8.2). The Panel did note at the same time that Art. 19.1 DSU authorized it to suggest ways in which the Member concerned could bring its measure into conformity. With regard to Mexico's request concerning revocation, the Panel stated that, since it had concluded that the entire investigation rested on an insufficient basis and therefore never should have been initiated:

> we suggest that Guatemala revoke the existing anti-dumping measure on imports of Mexican cement, because, in our view, this is the only appropriate means of implementing our recommendation. (§ 8.6).

The same issue came up again during the proceedings of *Guatemala – Cement II*. Mexico again requested revocation of duties and reimbursement of illegally perceived duties. The Panel repeated its position that it had discretion to provide for suggestions, even in presence of a specific request by the complaining party to this effect (§ 9.5). It then went on to briefly remind the particular circumstances of the case at hand: the investigation should have never been initiated on the basis of the available information; illegalities were committed during the investigation; no finding that dumping occurred which caused injury was supported by the available evidence (§ 9.6). In light of all this, the Panel could:

> not perceive how Guatemala could properly implement our recommendation without revoking the anti-dumping measure at issue in this dispute. (§ 9.6)

The Panel report in *Argentina – Poultry Antidumping Duties* faced the same issue, that is, a request from Brazil to suggest revocation of the Argentine order imposing antidumping duties. The Panel had previously found that Argentina had violated its obligations:

(a) by determining that there was sufficient evidence to initiate an investigation when this was not the case;

(b) by having recourse to best information available in violation of Art. 6.8 AD;

(c) by making an improper comparison between normal value and export price;

(d) by failing to make an objective examination of the injury factors; and

(e) by de-respecting the causality-requirement.

---

[17] See also the Panel report in *US – Softwood Lumber IV (Article 21.5)* at § 5.6.

In the Panel's view, in light of the extent of Argentina's violations, a revocation of duties imposed was well in order (§§ 8.5ff.). In *Mexico – Steel Pipes and Tubes*, the Panel found that Mexico had violated a series of provisions referring to various stages of the investigation, and thus, revocation of duties was appropriate remedy (§§ 8.12–13). In its report on *US – 1916 Act (Japan)*, the Panel, although it recognized that the remedy that Japan requested it to suggest (that the US repeal its law found to be inconsistent with the WTO) was not the only way that the US could bring its measures into compliance (since, the panel itself accepts that an amendment of the law could probably suffice), it still went on to make the suggestion as requested by Japan, noting that its suggestion should be understood as one of the ways in which the US could bring its measures into conformity with the WTO (§ 6.292). The Panel report in *EC – Export Subsidies on Sugar* is the only case so far where a Panel suggested, although it was not requested to do so by the complaining parties. It justified its decision to offer a suggestion by underscoring the interests of the many developing countries participating in the process (§§ 8.3–5).

In *US – Anti-dumping Measures on OCTG*, the AB faced a challenge by Mexico to the effect that the Panel had violated its obligations under Art. 11 DSU by refusing to suggest when requested to do so (§§ 8.15–18). The AB rejected this argument, holding that Panels have discretion to suggest and are not required to do so (§ 189).[18]

All reports so far have consistently held that suggestions are not binding on their addressees, who can legitimately choose another (than the suggested) way to implement the recommendation addressed to them. In *EC – Bananas III (Article 21.5 – Ecuador) (Second Recourse)*, the AB went one step further and held that implementing a suggestion creates no presumption that compliance has been achieved (§ 325).

5.3 Recommendations, Suggestions and Remedies

The discussion above points to the conclusion that Panels only sparingly have issued suggestions, and even then, they were quick to underline that they were not intruding too much into the addressee's policy space, since suggestions anyway are not binding.

---

[18] Note, that with respect to export subsidies, there is an explicit requirement in the SCM Agreement that they must be withdrawn without delay. In such cases, the recommendation to bring the measures into compliance will be accompanied by a request that the export subsidy be withdrawn without delay (Art. 4.7 SCM). The AB in *US – FSC (Article 21.5 – EC)* stated that a defense to the effect that citizens have a right for an orderly transition cannot validly be raised against the obligation to withdraw immediately an illegal subsidy (§§ 223–224 and 229).

Lack of (binding) suggestions can lead of course to disagreements regarding implementation, a question that we discuss *infra*. Disagreements must be brought before "compliance Panels", and thus, the process is prolonged. This is the price that WTO Members are prepared to pay in order to guarantee maximum discretion regarding implementation of Panels' and AB rulings.

To the purist, this is particularly troublesome since extending the whole process by a few months equals additional damage for the complainant: this is so since we de facto live in a world of "prospective remedies" within the WTO. Few Members nevertheless have complained about it. A trade-off thus emerges between "compulsory third party adjudication", and "benign remedies". Rulings, we dare argue, serve more as guidelines for future behavior, rather than mechanisms for compensating damages suffered because of the commission of an illegal act.

6. Compliance

6.1 Punishing Deviations in the WTO

There are three necessary (albeit, not sufficient) prerequisites that must be fulfilled, for compliance to be achieved:

(a) A complaint has been introduced;

(b) The defendant has lost;

(c) The defendant has modified its policies/measures.

This last point needs some additional explanation. On purpose we did not include the term "illegality" in the discussion so far. A WTO Member can be requested to pay compensation even for doing nothing wrong, if, as a result of an un-anticipated (by its partners) legal action that it has undertaken, the value of its tariff concessions has been diminished. These are the conditions that case law has consistently attached for a non-violation complaint (NVC) to be successfully invoked.[19]

Now, why did we mention that these three conditions are necessary but not sufficient? Compliance can occur for many reasons: political economy ("use GATT as an excuse"), side payments (promise to vote for the complying party in another forum), reputation costs (for those who care), credibility of the threat in case of non-compliance. More often than not the rationale for complying is a question of private information. Only the parties to the dispute (or on occasion only the defendant itself) might know what deal has been sealed behind closed doors.

---

[19] NVCs represent a sizeable proportion of all disputes submitted to the WTO, see Horn *et al.* (2011).

Unfortunately, there seem to be little incentive for WTO Members to disclose such information regarding details of negotiated settlements. And such opacity might lead to certain opportunistic behavior.[20]

Therefore a comprehensive study regarding compliance in the WTO will prove to be a quixotic test. Though many are totally uninteresting for the discussion here. The issue is whether the WTO system itself induces compliance and not whether for reasons unrelated to it compliance has occurred.

WTO Members might wish to deviate from their obligations for a variety of reasons. A temporary (illegal) safeguard might persuade swing voters to vote for those in power. A (discriminatory) favor might incite equally cooperative behavior etc.

How does the WTO regime incite its Members to avoid such behavior? In case of deviation, Art. 22.4 DSU calls for equivalence between the proposed level of suspension of concessions and the level of nullification and impairment (damage) suffered by the injured party. The WTO regime aims to stop cheating some years after it has been committed (to be precise, from the end of the reasonable period of time during which compliance must occur: there is standing case law to this effect).

As to the mechanics, suffice to say that Art. 22.1 DSU explicitly reveals a preference for specific performance of the obligations assumed ("property rules"), "liability rules" (e.g., suspension of concessions) being relegated to a transitional instrument only.[21] Compensation and suspension of concessions or other obligations are temporary means that can be used alternatively until specific performance (and thus, resolution of the dispute) has been secured.

Compensation is voluntary. Its form is not prejudged in the DSU. It has only been agreed once. Following the condemnation of US copyright practices in US – Section 110(5) Copyright Act, the EU (complainant) and the US (defendant) agreed to submit to an Art. 25 DSU arbitration, since, they could not agree on the amount of compensation to be paid.[22] Case law has consistently held that:

(a) Remedies are prospective (which means there is no obligation to pay back damage inflicted from its commission until the end of the reasonable period of time for compliance);[23]

---

[20] Collins-Williams and Wolfe (2010) make a persuasive case why incentives drive the quantity and quality of notifications.

[21] See also Art. 22.8 DSU.

[22] Grossman and Mavroidis (2003).

[23] Petersmann (1993) refers to five GATT cases where retroactive remedies had been recommended. The DSU is silent on this issue: prospective remedies are a creation of WTO case law. With one exception all WTO Panels have recommended them.

(b) Indirect benefits cannot be recouped;

(c) Only value added matters;

(d) Legal fees cannot be recouped.

Retaliation on the other hand must of course, go beyond effectuating restitution if it is to discourage future exploitation. It must leave the opportunist clearly worse off than before the act of opportunism. If the sanction makes the victim whole, then as long as the opportunist is undetected for some time, it pays to continue to engage in opportunistic exploitation.

6.2 Deviations for All?

WTO Members do not share the same capacity to detect deviations.[24] The most powerful between them can rely on a highly diversified export portfolio and consequential presence of trade diplomacy around the globe. The weaker nations cannot rely on the TPRM (Trade Policy Review Mechanism), as they cannot rely on the notification system either. The former offers scattered information on periodic basis, whereas the record of notifications of national measures is good only when notifications are incentive compatible.[25]

In the absence of centralized enforcement,[26] those with the more sophisticated administrations will be in better position to detect deviations and act, if they deem it appropriate, faster reducing thus the period of impunity for deviators.

6.3 Punishing is an Investment Decision

Assuming detection, the decision to punish recalcitrant WTO Members is costly. Facing non-compliance, WTO Members can suspend concessions in order to encourage WTO-consistent behavior. The Arbitrators in *EC – Bananas III (Article 22.6 – US)* echoing many prior reports held that the purpose of countermeasures, as stated in Art. 22.1 DSU, is to induce compliance by the recalcitrant WTO Member (§6.3):

---

[24] The private sector can of course detect illegal trade barriers. It does not have standing before the WTO. It will have to "persuade" its government to act on its behalf, and it is political economy consideration that will decide whether to act upon similar complaints or not.

[25] While most commentators celebrate the record before the TBT and the SPS Committee, they deplore the record before the ILC and the SCM Committees, see Collins-William and Wolfe (2010).

[26] Hoekman and Mavroidis (2000).

Accordingly, the authorization to suspend concessions or other obligations is a temporary measure pending full implementation by the Member concerned. We agree with the United States that this temporary nature indicates that it is the purpose of countermeasures to *induce compliance*. (Emphasis in the original).

While suspending concessions, enforcers make life costlier for them since there are undeniable negative implications for consumer welfare. The investment will thus take place in the hope of recoupment when the illegality has ended. But the investor cannot hope for more than the re-establishment of the status quo ante anyway since there is statutory language providing for equivalence between damage and countermeasures. Moreover, because de facto we live in a WTO world of prospective remedies, the investor cannot be reimbursed for damage suffered until compliance has been achieved. Other things equal, these factors would argue for sub-optimal enforcement.

With this caveat, the intensity of inducement to comply is a function of the credibility of the threat. It is one thing for the EU to be excluded from the Ecuadorian market and yet quite another from Ecuador to be excluded from the EU market.

Finally, compliance can be induced on grounds unrelated to WTO. "Big" guys have more "persuasive" power in that they have more weapons to use when they decide to retaliate which, as Bernheim and Whinston (1990) have shown increases their retaliatory power.

6.4 Still, Should we Celebrate?

There are studies regarding aspects of compliance (that is, they look for example how often recourse to suspension of concessions occurred and between who and who and on what subject-matter). There are studies regarding particular disputes from A to Z, that is, they also discuss compliance in a particular case.

The problem with the former is that they are not informative enough as to the intensive margin, and with the latter that they offer little evidence regarding the extensive margin. Two studies to our knowledge do not suffer from similar vices: Davey (2007), and Bagwell *et al.* (2005). And yet, none of these studies address the question whether compliance was the result (the effect) of the mechanism that the DSU has put in place.[27]

The study by Bagwell *et al.* (2005) is probably better suited for our discussion here. They divide the WTO world between OECD (Organization of Economic Co-operation) and non-OECD members and then ask the question what has been the attitude of complainants

---

[27] Probably because as noted above we often lack information why compliance occurred.

when faced with non-compliance by the defendant. They identify a number of cases (less than twenty), where a non-OECD complainant is faced with non-compliance by the OECD defendant, (cases where the WTO was not notified of a change in policy), and yet the complainant did not go ahead and suspend concessions. On the other hand, they find no case where an OECD complainant has had to exercise threat (by suspending concessions) in order to induce compliance by a non-OECD defendant. This observation falls squarely within Schelling's (1960) classic account that for the threat to be credible, it does not have to be exercised. Once again, and in order to avoid misunderstandings, we are in the dark as to the reasons why losing non-OECD defendants opt for a change of their condemned policies. But this study seems to provide some empirical proof that bargaining asymmetries might matter when it comes to discussing compliance at the WTO. The identity of the parties to the dispute must be a key component in this discussion.

6.5 *Root and Branch Reformers, Hold Your Fire*

Against this background, proposals have been tabled on issues that have been resolved in practice (sequencing), or on issues of secondary importance (remand authority for the Appellate Body). There is talk on enforcement as well. Some, like proposals for monetary compensation, are in the wrong direction since similar proposals do not address the question: what if the defendant does not pay? The same holds for proposals to secure "partial" compliance, "total" being equated to a return to the *status quo ante*.

There are some proposals that aims to address asymmetric bargaining power across WTO Members: tradable remedies (not on the table anymore); linking right to vote/submit a dispute to prior compliance etc. They have not managed to gather pace since "across the floor" alliances are not easy.

There are other mechanisms that can help address this issue and there are examples as well: the EU has addressed the issue of asymmetric bargaining power across its members by introducing centralized enforcement. It is at least doubtful however, whether a total recall of the current regime is on the cards.

7. Concluding Remarks

The WTO dispute settlement system has lots of things to brag about. First and foremost, because of the process itself: this is the only genuine, comprehensive compulsory third party adjudication regime in international relations. Romans prided themselves for introducing widespread "*nemo judex in causa sua*". WTO is today's Rome in this respect.

Second, because the regime has managed to retain the confidence shown. It has attracted record numbers of disputes over the years, the proliferation of preferential trade agreements (PTAs) notwithstanding. Indeed, PTA partners routinely prefer to submit their disputes to the WTO rather than to their own, private forum.

This does not mean that the regime established is seamless, that criticism is by definition unwarranted. In this paper, we have argued that there are probably good reasons to tone down the celebratory pronouncements expressed ad nauseam by dozens of analysts regarding the high rate of compliance at the WTO. We also pointed to two areas where improvements are in order: first, the selection of WTO judges, and second, remedies. It is beyond the scope of this paper to advance concrete, elaborate proposals. To do that, one would need to "marry" different, and often conflicting considerations. We stop at the diagnosis-level, and the picture established *supra* is cause for concern.

References

Bagwell, Kyle, Petros C. Mavroids, and Robert W. Staiger. 2005. The Case for Tradable Remedies in WTO Dispute Settlement System, pp. 395–414 in Simon J. Evenett and Bernard M. Hoekman (eds.), *Economic Development & Multilateral Trade Cooperation*, Palgrave McMillan & The World Bank: Washington DC.

Bernheim, Douglas B. and Michael Whinston. 1990. *Multimarket Contact and Collusive Behavior*, RAND, 21, 1–26.

Collins-Williams, Terry, and Robert Wolfe. 2010. Transparency as Trade Policy Tool: the WTO's Cloudy Windows, *The World Trade Review*, 9: 551–581.

Davey, William J. 2007. Evaluating WTO Dispute settlement: What Results Have Been Achieved Through Consultations and Implementation of Panel Reports? pp. 98–140 in Y. Taniguchi, A. Yanovich, and J. Bohanes (eds.), *The WTO in the 21ˢᵗ century: Dispute Settlement, Negotiations, and Regionalism*, Cambridge U. Press: Cambridge, UK.

Elsig, Manfred and Mark A. Pollack. 2014. Agents, trustees, and international courts: The politics of judicial appointment at the World Trade Organization, *European Journal of International Relations*, 20: 391–415.

Grossman, Gene M., and Petros C. Mavroidis. 2003. Would've or Should've? Impaired Benefits Due to Copyright Infringement, pp. 294–314 in Henrik Horn, and Petros C. Mavroidis (eds.), *The American Law Institute Reporters' Studies on WTO Case Law*, Cambridge U. Press: New York.

Hoekman, Bernard M., and Petros C. Mavroidis. 2000. WTO Dispute Settlement, Transparency and Surveillance, *The World Economy*, 23: 527–542.

Horn, Henrik, Louise Johannesson, and Petros C. Mavroidis. 2011. The WTO Dispute Settlement System (1995–2010): Some Descriptive Statistics, *Journal of World Trade*, 45: 1107–1138.

Horn, Henrik, and Petros C. Mavroidis. 2014. Multilateral Environmental Agreements in the WTO: Silence Speaks Volumes, *International Journal of Economic Theory*, 10: 147–165.

Hudec, Robert E. 1993. *Enforcing International Trade Law*, Butterworths, London, UK.

Mavroidis, Petros C., and Mark Wu. 2012. *The Law of the WTO*, WEST Publishing: Egan, Minnesota.

Petersmann, Ernst-Ulrich. 1993. International Competition Rules for the GATT – MTO World Trade and Legal System, *Journal of World Trade*, 27: 35–86.

Schelling, Thomas. 1960. *The Strategy of Conflict*, Harvard U. Press: Cambridge, Mass.

Strengths, Weaknesses, Opportunities and Threats of Investor-State Dispute Settlement as Compared to WTO Dispute Settlement

Freya BAETENS[1]

I. Introduction

For centuries, individuals who had been injured by a foreign State and who wished to see that State being held responsible had to rely on the system of diplomatic protection, defined as "invocation by a State, through diplomatic action or other means of peaceful settlement, of the responsibility of another State for an injury caused by an internationally wrongful act of that State to a natural or legal person that is a national of the former State with a view to the implementation of such responsibility".[2]

However, the exercise of such diplomatic protection was a discretionary right of the State, not a right of the injured individual, who, as a result, had to persuade its home State to sue the foreign State for the violation of its obligations. This system had its obvious downsides, ranging from the fact that it fell entirely within the political appreciation of the home State to decide whether to espouse the claim, to the loss of control over the claim and its potential settlement, and finally to the lack of any obligation on the part of the claimant State to share any eventually-obtained compensation with the injured individual.

By contrast there is no equivalent to diplomatic protection in the World Trade Organization (WTO) dispute settlement system. Although the immediately injured parties of WTO-inconsistent measures may well be private companies or industries, the interests protected by the WTO system are the compliance interests of the WTO Members arising from

[1] Freya Baetens (*Cand./Lic.Jur. (Ghent); LL.M. (Columbia); Ph.D. (Cambridge)*) is Associate Professor of Law and Director of the LUC Research Centre at Leiden University and Visiting Professor at the National University Singapore (NUS). As a member of the Brussels Bar, she regularly acts as counsel or expert in international disputes. She is grateful for the feedback received from the participants at the Colloquium on "*The WTO Dispute Settlement Mechanism: A Health-Check*" at the College of Europe on 12 September 2014.
[2] Article 1, UN ILC "Draft Articles on Diplomatic Protection" (2006) GAOR 61st Session Supp 10, 16 (ILC Articles on Diplomatic Protection).

their participation in world trade – and the standing rules of the WTO as well as its remedial provisions reflect this.

As international law developed throughout the 20th century, alternatives to the system of diplomatic protection were established, most prominently in the form of human rights law (for example, via regional human rights courts) and international investment law. Under the latter system, investor-State dispute settlement (ISDS) gives foreign investors direct access to international remedies, or in other words, private standing to sue host States before international arbitral tribunals. ISDS may be regulated by different sets of procedural rules often linked to particular registry offices such as the International Centre for the Settlement of Investment Disputes (ICSID), the Permanent Court of Arbitration (PCA), the London Court of International Arbitration (LCIA) or the Stockholm Chamber of Commerce (SCC). The majority of investment arbitration claims have been brought under the Convention on the Settlement of Disputes between States and Nationals of Other States (ICSID Convention).[3] Other regimes include the ICSID Additional Facility Rules,[4] the UNCITRAL Arbitration Rules,[5] the International Chamber of Commerce (ICC) Rules,[6] the PCA Rules,[7] the LCIA Rules[8] and the SCC Rules.[9]

Regardless of the institutional framework under which investor-State claims are brought, ISDS proceedings share some common features, which may be modified by the terms of the particular International Investment Agreement (IIA) which provides for ISDS. In this Chapter, the ISDS system is scrutinized in light of the following five key elements: (1) appointment and functioning of arbitrators; (2) terms of reference; (3) policy space; (4) support mechanisms, and, (5) remedies and compliance.

---

[3]   Convention on the Settlement of Investment Disputes between States and Nationals of Other States (opened for signature 18 March 1965, entered into force 14 October 1966) 575 UNTS 159 (ICSID Convention).

[4]   ICSID Additional Facility Rules, ICSID/11/Rev. 1 (January 2003).

[5]   UNCITRAL Arbitration Rules, (with new article 1, paragraph 4, as adopted in 2013, UN Doc. UNGA Res. 68/109 (16 December 2013)). (UNCITRAL Rules).

[6]   ICC Rules of Arbitration, ICC publication 808, (Entered into force 1 January 1998), available at: <http://www.iccwbo.org/products-and-services/arbitration-and-adr/arbitration/icc-rules-of-arbitration/> (ICC Rules).

[7]   Permanent Court of Arbitration, Arbitration Rules (2012), (Effective 17 December 2012). Available at: <http://www.pca-cpa.org/showpagecafe.html?pag_id=1188>.

[8]   London Court of International Arbitration, Arbitration Rules (2014), (Effective 1 October 2014). Available at: <http://www.lcia.org/Dispute_Resolution_Services/lcia-arbitration-rules-2014.aspx>.

[9]   Stockholm Chamber of Commerce, Arbitration Rules (2010), (adopted by the Stockholm Chamber of Commerce and in force as of 1 January 2010). Available at: <http://sccinstitute.com/dispute-resolution/rules/> (SCC Rules).

II. Five Key Elements of ISDS

1. *Appointment and functioning of arbitrators*

(a) *Appointment procedure*

The vast majority of cases are governed procedurally by the ICSID or UNCITRAL Arbitration Rules, under both of which it is initially for the parties to the dispute to appoint the arbitrators.[10] ISDS tribunals are nearly always composed of three arbitrators. The standard arbitrator selection process works as follows: each party appoints an arbitrator while the third, who serves as the president, is appointed by agreement of the parties[11] or by the two party-appointed arbitrators.[12] In case no agreement can be reached, most IIAs provide for a default appointing authority such as the President of the International Court of Justice,[13] the Secretary-General of the PCA[14] or the President of the World Bank.[15]

(b) *Impartiality and independence*

All sets of procedural rules demand arbitrators' impartiality and independence[16] (including those that are party-appointed) while ICSID additionally requires expertise in "law, commerce, industry or finance".[17] Arbitrators have to provide a disclosure letter disclosing any potential or actual conflict of interests before being formally appointed.[18] If one party doubts whether any arbitrator complies with this requirement, it may challenge the appointment.[19] Grounds for such challenges can be

---

[10]   Note that dispute settlement centers such as ICSID, ICC and SCC may appoint their own arbitrators under circumstances.

[11]   Article 37, ICSID Convention.

[12]   Article 9(1) UNCITRAL Arbitration Rules.

[13]   Yearbook of the International Court of Justice (2011-2012), No. 66, at 154 (2012). See for example: Agreement Between Bosnia And Herzegovina And The Republic Of India For The Promotion And Protection Of Investments, (opened for signature 12 September 2006, entered into force 13 February 2008), available at: <http://investmentpolicyhub.unctad.org/IIA/CountryBits/96>.

[14]   B.W. Daly, *The Permanent Court of Arbitration*, in L.A. Mitselis and L. Shore (eds.), Arbitration Rules – International Institutions (3rd ed.), (Juris Publishing, 2010); see for example Agreement between Australia and the Lao People's Democratic Republic on the Reciprocal Promotion and Protection of Investments (Vientiane, 6 April 1994, entered into force on 8 April 1995) [1995] ATS 9.

[15]   Article 38 ICSID Convention; C. Giorgetti, Litigating International Investment Disputes: A Practitioner's Guide 149 (Brill Nijhoff, 2014).

[16]   Article 14(1) ICSID Convention; Article 14 SCC Rules; Article 11 UNCITRAL Arbitration Rules; Article 11(1) ICC Rules.

[17]   Article 14(1) ICSID Convention.

[18]   Rule 6(2) ICSID Arbitration Rules; Article 11 UNCITRAL Arbitration Rules.

[19]   Article 57 ICSID Convention; Articles 12-13 UNCITRAL Arbitration Rules.

found for example the International Bar Association Rules and include, but are not limited to, undisclosed interests such as shares in the investing company concerned, or, having extended advice to the respondent State in related matters (or even unrelated matters, at least if shortly before the case at hand).

Depending on the applicable procedural rules, a decision on the challenge will need to be taken either by the appointing authority or, in the case of ICSID, the other members of the Tribunal, before the main case can proceed.[20] If the challenge is successful or if the arbitrator resigns before such decision is issued, a new arbitrator will need to be appointed. Parties can bring such challenge throughout the entire case, although if a party has knowledge of certain facts and does not act within a reasonable time, it will be held to have lost its opportunity.[21] Should any evidence of bias be discovered after the decision has been rendered, it may be possible to have the award annulled under the ICSID annulment system, or set aside under the New York Convention.[22] Under the latter, but not the former, there is also the possibility of resisting enforcement of the award in courts elsewhere than the place of arbitration.

(c) Criticism

Some commentators have questioned arbitrators' independence towards investors[23] while some countries such as, Bolivia, Ecuador and Venezuela have invoked – *inter alia* – *bias towards investors* in international arbitration as grounds for their withdrawal from the ICSID Convention. Likewise, concerns have been expressed by UNCTAD regarding arbitrators' conflicts of interest.[24] On the one hand, it has been

---

[20] Article 58 ICSID Convention; Articles 13(4) UNCITRAL Arbitration Rules.

[21] The reasoning behind this is to avoid that a party acquires certain knowledge but waits to bring a challenge until, for example, a decision on preliminary measures or jurisdiction has been taken. See *Azurix Corp. v. Argentina*, ICSID Case No. ARB/01/12, Decision on the Application for Annulment of the Argentine Republic (1 September 2009); *CEMEX Caracas Investments B.V. and CEMEX Caracas II Investments B.V. v. Venezuela*, ICSID Case No. ARB/08/15, Decision on the Respondent's Proposal to Disqualify a Member of the Tribunal (6 November 2009); *CDC Group plc v. Republic of Seychelles*, ICSID Case No. ARB/02/14, Decision of the Ad Hoc Committee on the Application for Annulment of the Republic of Seychelles (29 June 2005).

[22] Article 62 ICSID Convention; Article V, Convention on the Recognition and Enforcement of Foreign Arbitral Awards (opened for signature 10 June 1958, entered into force 7 June 1959) 330 UNTS 38 (New York Convention).

[23] G. van Harten, *Perceived Bias in Investment Treaty Arbitration*, in M. Waibel *et al.* (eds.), The Backlash Against Investment Arbitration: Perceptions and Reality, 433 at 434 (Kluwer Law International, 2010).

[24] UNCTAD, IIA Issues Note, *Recent Developments in Investor-State Dispute Settlement (ISDS)* (2013), available at: <http://unctad.org/en/PublicationsLibrary/webdiaepcb2013d3_en.pdf>.

argued that the rules concerning impartiality and independence have been designed after commercial arbitration rules[25] and thus do not take due account of a State being a party to the dispute. Arbitrators with a competence on private/commercial law have been criticized as being unable to accommodate public interest concerns. On the other hand, one could equally argue that there may be a potential bias on the part of domestic courts, which would alternatively handle investor-State cases. Indeed, the sensitive and at times highly political character of the cases at issue could well result in judicial loyalty to the forum State, as the *Loewen* case[26] suggests.

Furthermore, arbitrators are said to be *not accountable* in that they do not belong to a permanent institution nor is there an authority to scrutinize their actions as distinct from their award. Such a "democratic deficit" in the ISDS process could be viewed as alarming considering that the broad interpretative powers of arbitrators may give rise to large amounts of compensation to be paid by the respondent State.[27] However, arbitrators are accountable in the sense that, unlike most domestic court judges, they have to be reappointed for each case. Arbitrators tend to be highly aware of the need to be (and be seen as) unbiased in order not to jeopardize future appointments.[28]

Finally, *ad hoc* appointments have the inevitable effect of varied compositions of tribunals and arbitral awards thus arguably *lack consistency*.[29] However, tribunals have shown considerable eagerness to consider precedents and their awards often detail at length how the present decision logically flows from previous case law. In case prior decisions are not followed, tribunals have reasoned at length why it was necessary, in their particular case, to deviate from accepted practice.[30]

---

[25] Van Harten, *supra* note 23, at 378; A. Kulick, Global Public Interest in International Investment Law 13 (Cambridge University Press, 2012).

[26] *The Loewen Group, Inc. and Raymond L. Loewen v. United States of America*, ICSID Case No. ARB(AF)/98/3, Award (26 Jun 2003). In the *Loewen* case, the arbitral tribunal held that the rights of a Canadian investor had been violated by US courts. In paragraph 137, the tribunal found that "the whole trial and its resultant verdict were clearly improper and discreditable and cannot be squared with minimum standards of international law and fair and equitable treatment", although the claim was fortuitously held inadmissible on other grounds.

[27] S.W. Schill, *Enhancing International Investment Law's Legitimacy: Conceptual and Methodological Foundations of a New Public Law Approach*, 52 Virginia Journal of International Law 57, at 66 (2011).

[28] C. Tietje & F. Baetens, *The Impact of Investor-State Dispute Settlement (ISDS) in the Transatlantic Trade and Investment Partnership*, at 68 (2014) (Tietje & Baetens).

[29] H. Mann, "Transparency and Consistency in International Investment Law: can the Problems be fixed by Tinkering?", in *Appeals Mechanism in International Investment Disputes*, ed. by Karl P. Sauvant; with Michael Chiswick-Patterson (OUP 2008) 213-221.

[30] M. Ewing-Chow, "Coherence, Convergence and Consistency in International Investment Law", in *Prospects in International Investment Law and Policy: World*

(d) Current developments

Considerable developments are underway to reform the appointment and functioning of arbitrators, which is especially clear in ongoing FTA negotiations between the EU and the US concerning the Transatlantic Trade and Investment Treaty (TTIP).[31] The following elements in particular are considered: (1) the creation of a code of ethics for arbitrators; (2) a roster of arbitrators; and (3) an appeals mechanism.

A comprehensive *code of ethics* for arbitrators aims to regulate their conduct and guarantee impartiality. Such a code would be complemented by disqualification mechanisms in case of conflict of interest, no longer leaving this to the discretion of the appointing authority. If a code of ethics is coupled with a provision on arbitrators' expertise, it would produce optimal results. Setting competence in public international law and international investment law as a requirement for an arbitrator to be appointed would address concerns regarding their incapability of taking public law rationales into due account. Thus, uniform selection and qualification criteria for the constitution of the tribunal could afford the process with greater legitimacy.

Furthermore, the establishment of a *pre-agreed roster* from which arbitrators would be drawn could serve as an additional safeguard. Such roster would provide for an extensive list of widely-accepted qualified and specialized individuals capable of delivering equitable decisions. A large roster of arbitrators could take due account of an adequate geographical and gender distribution, as well as use a rotating system which ensures access of new arbitrators. In addition to avoiding the criticism that arbitration is a closed or even nepotistic system, it would also ensure that the appointed arbitrators do not have a multitude of simultaneously pending cases so they have sufficient time available to render their awards promptly.

Considerable care should be taken, however, that membership of such roster is indeed based on expertise in the relevant subject matter and not merit in other areas. The current proposal of the European Commission in the course of the TTIP negotiations even goes further in that it provides for a fixed tribunal, thereby abolishing the right of the parties to the dispute to choose their own judges.[32]

Trade Forum, ed. by R. Echandi and P. Sauvé, (CUP 2013) 228-235; C. Schreuer, "Coherence and Consistency in International Investment Law", in *Prospects in International Investment Law and Policy: World Trade Forum*, ed. by R. Echandi and P. Sauvé, (CUP 2013) 391-402.

[31] See the TTIP draft Investment Chapter, released on 12 November 2015, available at: <http://trade.ec.europa.eu/doclib/docs/2015/november/tradoc_153955.pdf>.

[32] Section 3, TTIP draft Investment Chapter, released on 12 November 2015, available at: <http://trade.ec.europa.eu/doclib/docs/2015/november/tradoc_153955.pdf>.

Finally, an *appeals mechanism* might offer an additional safety net as well as significantly increase the consistency of arbitral awards. The establishment of an appellate mechanism has been contemplated in a couple of FTAs concluded by the US, namely the US-Chile FTA (2003) and the Dominican Republic-Central America-US FTA (CAFTA-DR) (2004), as well as in the current TTIP draft,[33] but such a body has not yet been constituted. The existing annulment proceedings under ICSID are limited in scope, as they only concern the legitimacy of the process under exhaustive grounds (not a review of the case on its merits)[34] while the result of the annulment is the removal of the award which may be resubmitted to a new tribunal, not its replacement. Thus, ICSID annulment mechanism is not considered as an appellate facility.

The WTO Appellate Body (AB) could serve as an example for the establishment of an appeals facility in the field of international investment law. Like the WTO AB, an appeal institution should have competence to undertake a review of the points of law and legal interpretations of the first instance tribunal while time constraints would make the process expeditious. The latter would have to be ring-fenced by very tight timelines in order to prevent frivolous appeals that simply aim at prolonging the proceedings and increase the costs.[35] Such a mechanism could contribute to enlarging the limited pool of arbitrators who are currently appointed to arbitral tribunals because parties would probably "risk" appointing a somewhat less-experienced arbitrator, in the secure knowledge that, in case an unexpected award is rendered, they have the option to appeal.[36]

Yet, given the multilayered nature of international investment law with multiple BITs and FTAs, a standing appellate mechanism can only be considered at the level of one particular FTA or BIT. It would not be excluded (or even unlikely) that countries decide to make use of the same appellate system for all of their IIAs, for example, the EU could try to persuade all of its future investment treaty partners to adopt the system it is currently developing in the framework of the TTIP. Thus, although not comparable to the predictability of the WTO multilateral regime's interpretation by the WTO AB, a degree of coherence is expected to be achieved by an appellate facility established under certain (groups of) FTAs/BITs.

---

[33] Section 3, TTIP draft Investment Chapter, released on 12 November 2015, available at: <http://trade.ec.europa.eu/doclib/docs/2015/november/tradoc_153955.pdf>.

[34] Under Article 52 ICSID Convention: "*(1) Either party may request annulment of the award by an application in writing addressed to the Secretary-General on one or more of the following grounds: (a) that the Tribunal was not properly constituted; (b) that the Tribunal has manifestly exceeded its powers; (c) that there was corruption on the part of a member of the Tribunal; (d) that there has been a serious departure from a fundamental rule of procedure; or (e) that the award has failed to state the reasons on which it is based*".

[35] Tietje & Baetens, *supra* note 28, at 112.

[36] *Id.*, at 113.

2. Terms of reference

Most IIAs do not include a choice of law clause. Yet, when they do, they mostly provide that any dispute is to be governed "in accordance with the provisions of the Agreement",[37] while frequently the IIA is applicable in conjunction with "the principles of international law".[38] According to the principle of party autonomy in ISDS and insofar as allowed by the IIA, the applicable law to a dispute is selected by the disputing parties involved (*choice of law*), such selection being binding upon the tribunal.

Article 42(1) of the ICSID Convention provides that "the Tribunal shall decide a dispute in accordance with such *rules of law* as may be agreed by the parties" while Article 33(1) of the UNCTAD Arbitration Rules refers to "the *law* designated by the parties" as applicable in a certain dispute. References to "rules of law", as opposed to an entire legal system, such as law of the host State, general principles of law or international law, entail some flexibility and allow for a combination of sets of legal norms to occur.[39] For example, when it comes to obligations arising out of a contract, the law of the host State is likely to apply, sometimes in conjunction with international law.[40]

Only in the *absence of choice of law* will the arbitral tribunal have to exercise some discretion to determine the law to govern a dispute. In the absence of agreement between the parties on the choice of law, Article 42(1) of the ICSID Convention provides that "the Tribunal shall apply the law of the Contracting State party to the dispute (including its rules on the conflict of laws) and such rules of international law as may be applicable". Under Article 33(1) of the UNCITRAL Arbitration Rules "the arbitral tribunal shall apply the law determined by the conflict of laws rules which it considers applicable." Thus, contrary to the latter Rules, the ICSID Convention provides for obligatory parallel application of both the law of the host State and international law. As arbitral practice indicates, in most cases where the parties did not make a choice of law, arbitrators opted for the law of the host State whereas international law only applied when there were *lacunae* in the law of the host State or the law of the host State was inconsistent with international law or contrary to fundamental norms of international law.[41] In *Wena v. Egypt*,[42] the *ad hoc* Committee – after confirming that the meaning of Article 42(1)

---

[37] See, for example, BITs concluded by Australia, Belgium, Canada and Spain.

[38] See, for example, BITs concluded by Argentina, Chile, China and Costa Rica.

[39] See Y. Banifatemi, *The Law Applicable in Investment Treaty Arbitration*, *in* K. Yannaca-Small (ed.) Arbitration Under International Investment Agreements: A Guide to the Key Issues 191 at 196 (Oxford University Press, 2010).

[40] *Id.*

[41] *Id.*, at 201-202.

[42] *Wena Hotels Ltd. v. Egypt*, ICSID Case No. ARB/98/4, Decision on Application for Annulment (5 February 2002), 41 ILM 933 (2002).

is that the law of the host State may be applied in conjunction with international law – held that "so too international law can be applied by itself if the appropriate rule is found in this other ambit".[43] The latter case is instructive in that it was found that international law may apply alone – excluding the law of the host State – without the need of finding a *lacuna* or inadequacy of the latter.[44]

3. Amount of "policy space"

(a) Current situation

A-recurring criticism of international investment law is that it overly[45] limits sovereign regulatory powers of States to pursue public interest objectives, in order to over-protect foreign investors' interests. Preserving "policy" or "regulatory" space has been named by several Latin American countries (Bolivia, Ecuador, Venezuela) as one of the reasons for terminating their membership of the ICSID Convention and/or BITs.[46] Indonesia, Australia and South Africa have amended their IIA negotiation strategy and/or announced a review of their current BITs with the objective of renegotiation or termination for this reason. However, they have subsequently adopted new agreements including ISDS, so it would seem more of an *ad hoc* decision, rather than a comprehensive policy.[47]

Only a handful of cases raise core issues as to the extent to which governments maintain their policy space after concluding IIAs. But concerns were raised regarding the possibility of ISDS claims provoking

---

[43] *Id.*, at 941.

[44] Banifatemi, *supra* note 39, at 203.

[45] The question whether IIAs limit sovereign powers is moot as all treaties to some extent limit the regulatory (and other) freedoms of States to act exactly as they please.

[46] See C. Schreuer, *Denunciation of the ICSID Convention and Consent to Arbitration*, in Waibel *et al.* (eds.), *supra* note 23, 353.

[47] For example, the Japan-Australia Economic Partnership Agreement (JAEPA) signed in July 2014 does not include ISDS (containing however a clause in Article 14.19 which provides for the review of the JAEPA Investment Chapter, including the position with respect to an ISDS mechanism); See Agreement between Australia and Japan for an Economic Partnership, available at: <http://dfat.gov.au/trade/agreements/jaepa/official-documents/Documents/jaepa-chapters-1-to-20.pdf>. However the Transpacific Partnership which includes both Australia and Japan does provide for ISDS (Chapter 9, Section B, the TPP was concluded on 5 Oct 2015, available at <https://medium.com/the-trans-pacific-partnership/investment-c76dbd892f3a#.vxgwcon50>); See also L.E. Trakman, *Choosing Domestic Courts over Investor-State Arbitration: Australia's Repudiation of the Status Quo* 35 UNSW Law Journal 979 (2012); B. Bland, "Indonesia to Terminate More Than 60 Bilateral Investment Treaties", Financial Times (26 March 2014), available at: <http://www.ft.com/cms/s/0/3755c1b2-b4e2-11e3-af92-00144feabdc0.html#axzz34QJuirDj>.

a political backlash concerning sensitive public regulation, especially in the light of the *Vattenfall v. Germany*[48] and *Phillip Morris v. Australia*[49] cases. The *Vattenfall* case concerns a claim brought by the Swedish energy company Vattenfall under the Energy Charter Treaty (ECT) asking for compensation because of the rapid change in German policy from extending permits for nuclear power plants and to suddenly withdrawing this decision only month later. This case is currently pending. This dispute follows an earlier one between the parties regarding environmental restrictions on a EUR 2.6 billion coal-fired power plant under construction which were introduced by the Government only after the initial permit was granted. This dispute was ultimately settled. In the *Phillip Morris* case, the tobacco company challenges the Australian Tobacco Plain Packaging Act 2011 under the Hong Kong-Australia BIT.[50] A similar case is brought by the same investor against the government of Uruguay.[51]

The representativeness of these cases should not be overstated: the large majority of investor-State arbitrations do not concern claims that certain policies, regulations or laws themselves violate States' obligations to protect foreign investors, but rather their (for example, discriminatory) implementation.[52] Current case law reveals that arbitral tribunals tend to rule in favor of respondent States when the latter have enacted non-discriminatory regulations in the public interest.[53] Furthermore, a 2014

---

[48]   *Vattenfall AB and others v. Germany*, ICSID Case No. ARB/12/12.

[49]   *Philip Morris Asia Limited v. Australia*, UNCITRAL, PCA Case No. 2012-12, Award (17 December 2015).

[50]   Furthermore, in 2013 several environment-related arbitrations have been initiated, including *Lone Pine Resources Inc. v. Canada*, ICSID Case No. UNCT/15/2; *Windstream Energy LLC v. Canada*, Permanent Court of Arbitration Case No. 2013-22, Award (27 September 2016); *Spence v. Costa Rica*, (ICSID Case No. UNCT/13/2), Interim Award (25 October 2016) and *Lieven J. van Riet, Chantal C. van Riet and Christopher van Riet v. Republic of Croatia*, ICSID Case No. ARB/13/12, Award (2 November 2016).

[51]   *Philip Morris Brands Sàrl, Philip Morris Products S.A. and Abal Hermanos S.A. v. Uruguay* (formerly *FTR Holding SA, Philip Morris Products S.A. and Abal Hermanos S.A. v. Uruguay*), ICSID Case No. ARB/10/7, Award (July 2016).

[52]   J. Caddel and N. Jensen, *Which Host Country Government Actors are Most Involved in Disputes with Foreign Investors?*, Columbia FDI Perspectives: Perspectives on Topical Foreign Direct Investment Issues by the Vale Columbia Center on Sustainable International Investment (No. 120, 28 April 2014), available at: <http://academiccommons.columbia.edu/catalog/ac:173529>; See also Tietje & Baetens, *supra* note 28, at 46-47.

[53]   See S.D. Franck, *Development and Outcomes of Investment Treaty Arbitration*, 50 Harvard International Law Journal 435, at 447 (2009). Note, for example, *Methanex Corporation v. United States of America*, UNCITRAL, Final Award of the Tribunal on Jurisdiction and Merits (3 August 2005); *Chemtura Corporation v. Canada*, UNCITRAL, Award (2 August 2010). However, see also earlier Metalclad case which ruled that the respondent State had no authority to deny the company's construction permit on environmental grounds; *Metalclad Corporation v. The United Mexican*

study concluded that the vast majority of ISDS claims arise from executive branch decisions (47% of disputes were associated with ministries or agencies) rather than legislative acts (amounting to 9% – 14 cases).[54] Thus, concerns that regulatory chill by domestic governments might be a side-effect of the inclusion of ISDS in IIAs should not be exaggerated.

(b) Potential safeguards

A set of safeguards to guide the interpretation of treaty provisions by tribunals could address the remaining concerns. First of all, *public policy carve-outs* that would reserve the right of governments to regulate in areas such as public health, the environment or labor could sufficiently address the intersection between investment and core public policy areas.[55] Referral to or incorporation of the Organisation for Economic Co-operation and Development (OECD) Guidelines on social corporate responsibility[56] and International Labor Organization (ILO) Declaration[57] could also be of value. Furthermore, the inclusion of other exceptions, such as prudential measures in the banking sector, but also essential security or taxation carve-outs, would not prevent States from closely regulating, say, financial service providers in order to ensure the stability of the financial sector and the protection of depositors.[58]

Regulatory space could also be preserved by *clarifying the scope of investment treaty standards*. Notions such as "fair and equitable treatment" (FET) or indirect expropriation are notorious for their vagueness which may result to expansive and inconsistent interpretations by arbitrators. Indeed, the FET principle has been, for example, characterized as lacking a "consolidated and conventional core meaning [or definition] that can

---

States, ICSID Case No. ARB(AF)/97/1, Award (30 August 2000). The decision now seems something of an outlier.

54 Caddel and Jensen, *supra* note 52.

55 Yet, such carve-outs have be carefully applied so they are not used as a guide to undermine treaty protections against discriminatory or inequitable measures; See A.D. Mitchell & J. Casben, *The National Interest in Trade and investment Agreements: Protecting the Health of Australians*, at 11 (2014), available at: <http://papers.ssrn.com/sol3/papers.cfm?abstract_id=2463061>.

56 OECD Guidelines for Multilateral Enterprises, 2011 Edition (OECD Publishing), available at: <http://www.oecd.org/daf/inv/mne/48004323.pdf>; see also International Chamber of Commerce (ICC), "ICC Guidelines for International Investment", at 18-19 (2012), available at: <http://www.iccwbo.org/Advocacy-Codes-and-Rules/Document-centre/2012/2012-ICC-Guidelinesfor-International-Investment/>; K. P. Sauvant & F. Ortino, *Improving the International Investment Law and Policy Regime: Options for the Future*, Ministry for Foreign Affairs of Finland, at 73-74 (2013).

57 ILO Declaration on Fundamental Principles and Rights at Work (1998), available at: <http://www.ilo.org/declaration/thedeclaration/textdeclaration/lang--en/index.htm>.

58 Tietje & Baetens, *supra* note 28, 100.

be applied easily".[59] The FET could be defined to comprise only the customary international law minimum standard of treatment – as has already been done by the NAFTA Free Trade Commission, for example, with regard to Article 1105 of NAFTA.[60] Indirect expropriation could exclude cases in which only a reduction of the value of the investment occurs, and could be defined so as to limit the types of government measures that could be successfully challenged.[61] Circumscription of key investment protection standards not only would provide sufficient guidance to tribunals but would also limit States' exposure to ISDS.[62]

Further control of the interpretative powers of tribunals could be achieved through *joint binding interpretations* by the parties to the IIA in question.[63] Such interpretations would confirm parties' intentions when drafting the treaty and clarify key investment concepts; most importantly, it would contribute to strengthening the predictability of decisions under very general norms such as "fair and equitable treatment" and "full protection and security".[64] In addition, an active role on the part of the State Parties to the treaty would take account of their "legitimate and ongoing interest in interpreting their own treaty obligations".[65] Optimally, joint interpretations be complemented by submission of *amicus curiae* briefs, including by NGOs, representatives of civil society and other third parties with a particular interest, such as industry federations.[66]

---

[59] S.W. Schill, The Multilateralization of International Investment Law, 155 (Cambridge University Press, 2009).

[60] See G. Clyde Hufbauer & J.J Schott, NAFTA Revisited: Achievements and Challenges 226 (Institute for International Economics, Washington, DC., 2005); Notes of Interpretation of Certain Chapter Eleven Provisions (Free Trade Commission, July 31, 2001), available at <http://www.international.gc.ca>. See also European Parliament Resolution of 6 April 2011 on the Future European International Investment Policy (2010/2203(INI)), para 19, available at: <http://www.europarl.europa.eu/sides/getDoc.do?pubRef=-//EP//NONSGML+TA+P7-TA-2011-0141+0+DOC+PDF+V0//EN>.

[61] Tietje & Baetens, *supra* note 28, at 101.

[62] *Id.*

[63] The inclusion of a provision on joint interpretations coupled with submissions by investor's home country has been proposed by the European Commission in the course of the TTIP negotiations; European Commission, Fact sheet: Investment Protection and Investor-to State Dispute Settlement in EU agreements, 26 November 2013, at 9, available at: <http://trade.ec.europa.eu/doclib/docs/2013/november/tradoc_151916.pdf>.

[64] See G. Kaufmann-Kohler, *Interpretive Powers of the Free Trade Commission and the Rule of Law* (2011), available at: <http://www.arbitrationicca.org/media/1/13571335953400/interpretive_powers_of_the_free_trade_commission_and_the_rule_of_law_kaufmann-kohler.pdf>.

[65] A. Roberts, *Clash of Paradigms: Actors and Analogies Shaping the Investment Treaty System*, at 23 (2012), available at: <http://www.iilj.org/courses/documents/Robertsclash.pdf>.

[66] *Amicus curiae* intervention has also been allowed in certain WTO and NAFTA proceedings; See, for example, *United States – Import Prohibition of Certain Shrimp and Shrimp Products*, WT/DS58/AB/R (6 November 1998), paras. 9-110; *United States – Definitive Safeguard Measures on Imports of Wheat Gluten from the European*

Finally, the inclusion of *"umbrella clauses"* in IIAs could be considered as unduly limiting governments' continuing right to regulate.[67] Many IIAs include such a clause which requires host States to observe any undertakings with regard to foreign investments, thus bringing obligations undertaken in contracts or other arrangements under the umbrella of protection of the IIA.[68] These "umbrella clauses" have the effect of elevating breaches of investors' contractual rights at the same level as breaches of investors' rights caused by administrative or legislative acts,[69] their elimination in future could be considered.

4. Support mechanisms

(a) Tribunal-appointed experts

UNCITRAL Rules of Arbitration (as well as ICC and LCIA Rules) explicitly grant arbitrators the power to appoint their own experts to provide a report on specific issues.[70] The ICSID Convention lacks an equivalent provision. In the absence of such, arbitrators have relied on Article 43 of the ICSID Convention according to which

> *"Except as the parties otherwise agree, the Tribunal may, if it deems it necessary at any stage of the proceedings,*
>
> *(a) call upon the parties to produce documents or other evidence, and*
>
> *(b) visit the scene connected with the dispute, and conduct such inquiries there as it may deem appropriate."*

The absence of a provision empowering tribunals to appoint experts under ICSID thus tends to confirm the more adversarial than inquisitorial nature of arbitration. The appointment of tribunal-appointed[71] experts in ISDS has been a rare practice, mostly associated with the assessment of damages.[72] The employment of technical and financial expertise in the

---

    Communities, WT/DSI66/AB/R (19 January 2001), at 168-176 and *Methanex Corporation v. United States of America*, UNCITRAL, Decision of the Tribunal on Petitions from Third Persons to Intervene as "Amici curiae" (3 August 2005).

[67] J.W. Salacuse, The Law of Investment Treaties 278 (Oxford University Press, 2009); See also Sauvant & Ortino, *supra* note 56, at 69-70.

[68] A. Newcombe & L. Paradell, Law and Practice of Investment Treaties: Standards of Treatment 437 (Kluwer Law International, 2009).

[69] R. Dolzer & M. Stevens, Bilateral Investment Treaties 81-82 (Kluwer Law International, 1995).

[70] Article 29(1) UNCITRAL Arbitration Rules; Article 25(4) ICC Rules; Article 21(1)(a) LCIA Rules.

[71] Note the difference with party-appointed experts.

[72] See, for example, *CMS Gas Transmission Co. v. Argentina*, ICSID Case No. ARB/01/8, Award (12 May 2005); *Sempra v. Argentina*, ICSID Case No. ARB/02/16, Award (28 Sep 2007); *Enron Corporation and Ponderosa Assets LP v. Argentina*, ICSID Case No. ARB/01/3, Award (22 May 2007).

course of the assessment of damages has apparently been considered as enhancing the legitimacy of the award's valuation.[73] Other useful reliance on experts could be found in assessments of the correct interpretation of national law or expertise with regard to the execution of scientific studies such as environmental impact assessment.

The *Abaclat* award[74] for example has been criticized because, in the absence of agreement between the parties on the appointment of an expert, the majority of the tribunal went ahead and appointed the expert in question nevertheless, stating that "based on Articles 43 and 44 of the ICSID Convention and Rules 19 and 34 of the ICSID Arbitration Rules and on past practice of various ICSID tribunals, it has competence to appoint an independent expert."[75] The dissenting arbitrator, as well as some commentators, vehemently disagreed,[76] on the ground that such appointments require the consent of the parties. This illustrates the debate concerning the level of control the parties should have in ISDS procedures.

(b) Tribunal secretaries and legal officers

In addition to organizing the practical organization of the arbitral proceedings (organizing meetings, hearings, exchange of correspondence, etc.), registry offices also offer legal support in the form of tribunal secretaries. In addition, tribunals may also wish to appoint a legal officer, similar to a *référendaire* at the Court of Justice of the EU or a law clerk in certain domestic courts, to assist with the drafting of the award. Parties are usually asked to agree to such appointment and these legal officers are often required to sign a confidentiality agreement, as they will be privy to all documents exchanged in the proceedings. However, their precise

---

[73] J. B. Simmons, *Valuation in Investor-State Arbitration: Towards a More Exact Science*, 30 Berkeley Journal of International Law 196, at 242 (2012).

[74] *Abaclat and Others v. Argentina (formerly Giovanna a Beccara and Others v. Argentina)*, ICSID Case No. ARB/07/5, Procedural Order No. 15 (20 November 2012). *Abaclat* case forms an exception in that the expert was not appointed for the valuation of damage but in order to examine information contained in a database including the details of the claimants; see paras. 19-38.

[75] *Id.*, para. 12.

[76] See *id.*, Dissenting Opinion of Dr. Torres Bernardez, paras. 44-45; R.J. Bettauer, Tribunal Establishes Initial Procedures for Review of Mass Bondholder Claims against Argentina, 17 ASIL Insight 16 (2013). For a broader critical analysis of this case see Cabrera C., Orlando F., The Freedom of Arbitrators to Conduct Collective Proceedings When the Rules are Silent: Considerations in the Wake of the Abaclat Decision, 6 Journal of International Dispute Settlement 1 (2015), 163-187; Kabra, R., Has Abaclat v Argentina left the ICSID with a massive problem?, 31 Arbitration International 3 (2015) 425-453; Aggerwal, M., Investment Treaty Arbitration Post-Abaclat: Towards a Taxonomy of Mass Claims, 3 Cambridge Journal of International and Comparative Law 3 (2014) 825-852.

role (the extent to which they may draft without specific instructions, whether they may be present during deliberations, etc.) is ambiguous and cause for naming them "the unofficial fourth arbitrators".[77]

5. *Remedies and compliance*

(a) *Usual remedy: monetary compensation*

In international investment arbitration, tribunals could in theory rely upon the whole gamut of options available under general international law in order to provide a remedy, from restitution to reparation in the form of compensation or satisfaction.[78] However, ISDS remedies almost invariably take the form of monetary compensation to reflect the damage that has been actually suffered by the victim, and not an order for a State to amend their conduct or law – which forms one of the major differences with WTO remedies.[79]

ISDS awards are usually final and binding upon the parties[80] and generally have a high compliance rate (with some notable high-publicity exceptions such as the Argentina cases);[81] although further research is needed on this.[82] The pecuniary obligations (unlike other remedies) imposed by *ICSID awards* are to be enforced like those arising from final domestic judgments in all States Parties to the ICSID Convention.[83] Given that enforcement may take place in any ICSID contracting party, the winning party may select a State where compliance is most likely to

---

[77] C. Partasides, The Fourth Arbitrator? The Role of Secretaries to Tribunals in International Arbitration, 18 Arbitration International 2 (2002) 147-163.

[78] *Case Concerning the Factory at Chorzow* (Germany v Poland), Judgment on the Merits, PCIJ, Series A, No.17, 4, 26 July 1927.

[79] M. Bronckers & F. Baetens, *Reconsidering financial remedies in WTO dispute settlement*, 18 *Journal of International Economic Law* 3 (2013) 281-311; ISDS remedies may, however, take the form of a certain performance requirement, such as disclosure of certain information, as well, see e.g., *Muhammet Çap & Sehil İnşaat Endustri ve Ticaret Ltd. Sti. v. Turkmenistan* (ARB/12/6) Provisional Measures Order (12 June 2015).

[80] Article 53 ICSID Convention. See also J.E. Kalicki & A. Joubin-Bret, Reshaping the Investor-State Dispute Settlement System 67 (2015); W.-M. Choi, *The Present and Future of the Investor-State Dispute Settlement Paradigm, in* W.J. Davey & J. Howard Jackson (eds.), The Future of International Economic Law 287 at 303 (2008). F. Baetens, *"'To ICSID or Not to ICSID' Is Not the Question"*, in I. A. Laird and T. J. Weiler, (eds.), Investment Treaty Arbitration and International Law – Volume 5 (Juris Publishing, 2012).

[81] See C. Tietje, *Perspectives on the Interaction Between International Trade and Investment Regulation*, in R. Echandi & P. Sauvé (eds.), Prospects in International Investment Law & Policy: World Trade Forum 166 at 169 (Cambridge University Press, 2013).

[82] A. Joubin-Bret, *Is There a Need For Sanctions in International Investment Arbitration?*, 160 American Society of International Law 130, ASIL Proceeding, at 130 (2012).

[83] Article 54 ICSID Convention.

succeed.[84] The enforcement procedures are governed by the law of the country where the execution takes place, but laws on State immunity against enforcement continue to apply.[85]

When it comes to *non-ICSID awards*, including those rendered under the ICSID Additional Facility Rules, enforcement is governed the New York Convention and by the national law of the State of enforcement.[86] This may imply such awards can be subjected to additional scrutiny[87] by the national courts in the State where enforcement is sought, but the outcome in practice (recognition and enforcement) is in the large majority of cases the same in effect as with ICSID awards. Even in case a domestic court would find that one of the conditions of the New York Convention is not met (for example, the arbitral panel was improperly constituted or the subject-matter was not capable for settlement via arbitration) and it refuses to enforce the award, the winning party can still attempt to enforce the award in another jurisdiction.

Importantly, *failure to comply* with ISDS awards may cause the investor's home State to exercise its right of diplomatic protection.[88] Although compliance with ISDS awards has generally not been problematic, non-compliance with two ISDS awards has given rise to the elevation of an ISDS case to the State-to-State level. In both cases the US government exercised a form of trade retaliation by opting

---

[84] R. Dolzer & C. Schreuer, Principles of International Investment Law 288 (Oxford University Press, 2008).

[85] Article 55 ICSID Convention.

[86] See M. Burgstaller, *European Law Challenged to Investment Arbitration, in* M. Waibel *et al.* (eds.), *supra* note 22, 455 at 473; M.I.M. Aboul-Enein, *Arbitration for Investment Disputes: Responses to the New Challenges and Changing Circumstances, in* A. J. van den Berg (ed.) New Horizons in International Commercial Arbitration and Beyond 181 at 188 (Kluwer Law International, 2005).

[87] Such scrutiny can take place on the following grounds: Article V(1): "*respondent may object: (a) The parties were under some incapacity, or the arbitration agreement is not valid; or (b) The party against whom the award is invoked was not given proper notice of the appointment of the arbitrator or of the arbitration proceedings or was otherwise unable to present his case; or (c) The award deals with a difference not contemplated by or not falling within the terms of the submission to arbitration, or it contains decisions on matters beyond the scope of the submission to arbitration, (d) The composition of the arbitral authority or the arbitral procedure was not in accordance with the agreement of the parties, or, with the law of the country where the arbitration took place; or (e) The award has not yet become binding on the parties, or has been set aside or suspended by a competent authority of the country in which, or under the law of which, that award was made.; Article V(2): court may* proprio motu *object: (a) The subject matter of the difference is not capable of settlement by arbitration under the law of that country; or (b) The recognition or enforcement of the award would be contrary to the public policy of that country*".

[88] Article 27 ICSID Convention. In ICSID cases, home States can no longer exercise their right to diplomatic protection, once an ISDS proceeding has been launched. In non-ICSID cases, there is no such explicit prohibition, although in practice, the home State would also refrain from exercising this right because it might be considered as prejudicial to the ISDS proceeding.

for the suspension of trade benefits under the General System of Preferences (GSP) Program for Argentina after the latter's failure to pay the compensation ordered by two awards rendered against it by ICSID tribunals.[89] Such a reaction by a home State government directly links ISDS to the WTO system and Article 22(2) DSU, in particular, which provides for possible suspension of concessions or other obligations, although it would be required first to obtain permission from the WTO Dispute Settlement Body for such action.

(b) Lack of compliance monitoring

The current institutional regime of international investment law lacks an institution to supervise compliance with ISDS awards or a sanctions system, equivalent to the WTO Trade Review system, but so far this has not seemed to cause particular problems. States' voluntary compliance with adverse awards is straightforwardly expected (and States generally live up to this expectation) given that it affirms their trustworthiness and signals to investors that the State in question honors its obligations. In sum, in the exceptional case of non-compliance, investors may either seek enforcement in other jurisdictions, or have recourse to their home State which may exercise diplomatic protection (which might lead to the submission of the dispute to the International Court of Justice) or impose unilateral sanctions on the non-complying State.

III. Conclusion: ISDS compared with WTO DS

The main weakness of ISDS is that it does not (yet) enjoy a relatively high degree of consistency and predictability compared with its WTO counterpart. This is largely due to the comprehensive multilateral treaty regime that the WTO dispute settlement institutions are to interpret in contrast to the patchwork of thousands of IIAs and resulting case law by a panoply of arbitral tribunals. Furthermore, the WTO Panel *and* Appellate Body review guarantee some degree of consistency which cannot be taken for granted in the case of ISDS. Also, contrary to ISDS, the WTO system provides for certain deadlines to be followed which makes the process expeditious.

Another substantial drawback of ISDS, not specifically touched upon in this paper, is the confidentiality of the process. Contrary to the WTO Reports, ISDS awards are not automatically published; rather publication is dependent on the consent of the parties. In the absence of a registry, comparable to that of the WTO, there have been some instances where

---

[89] Joubin-Bret, *supra* note 80, at 131.

either the content of awards or the very existence of an arbitration was never made available to the public (although this situation is becoming increasingly rare). The adoption of the 2013 UNCITRAL Transparency Rules is promising for a more transparent investment arbitration system, not merely in terms of the availability of awards but also access to the written and oral proceedings.[90] Finally, the WTO system also seems to provide for a clearer-regulated and less controversial system of Panel- and Appellate Body-appointed experts.

ISDS has a number of significant advantages (at least from a claimant perspective):[91] first of all, the injured parties are able to obtain (monetary) compensation, while an oft-heard criticism of the WTO system is that it can be quite attractive for a WTO Member to enact a non-compliant measure, keep it in force for a number of years during which another Member has to initiate consultations, after which a Panel and the Appellate Body have to issue a report.[92] When the Member subsequently voluntarily implements this report within a reasonable time, it may in fact have succeeded in sheltering part of its home industry for years against external competition, thereby irreparably injuring another Member's equivalent industry.

Moreover, the options that are open in case the losing Member does not voluntarily comply with the WTO report are rather meagre: compensation is possible after the reasonable time to implement has expired but only on a voluntary basis.[93] The only other remedy open to the injured WTO Member is to return to the Dispute Settlement Body and ask for permission to suspend "the application of concessions or other obligations under the covered agreements on a discriminatory basis vis-à-vis the other Member".[94] Even if such authorization is obtained, its coercive effect may be very limited, as illustrated for example by the suspensions by Antigua and Barbados after the US non-compliance in the *US – Gambling* case.[95]

---

[90] UNCITRAL Rules on Transparency in Treaty-Based Investor-State Arbitration (2014), (effective date 1 April 2014) available at: <https://www.uncitral.org/pdf/english/texts/arbitration/rules-on-transparency/Rules-on-Transparency-E.pdf>.

[91] ISDS provides for a significant degree of procedural flexibility. For example, under Rules 29 and 40 ICSID Arbitration Rules, parties may modify the procedures by agreement.

[92] See also Bronckers & Baetens, *supra* note 79.

[93] See, in general, R.R. Babu, Remedies Under the WTO Legal System 451-452 (Brill Nijhoff, 2012).

[94] Article 3(7), DSU, Dispute Settlement Rules: Understanding on Rules and Procedures Governing the Settlement of Disputes, Marrakesh Agreement Establishing the World Trade Organization, Annex 2, The Legal Texts: The Results Of The Uruguay Round Of Multilateral Trade Negotiations 354 (1999), 1869 UNTS. 401.

[95] *United States – Measures Affecting the Cross-Border Supply of Gambling and Betting Services*, WT/DS285/R (10 November 2004) and WT/DS285/AB/R (7 April 2005).

Furthermore, and in particular in case a violatory measure affects mostly one sector or even just a small number of companies, it could be questioned whether elevating such dispute to the inter-State level is the best way to solve it. Returning to the disadvantages attached to the diplomatic protection system enumerated in the introduction, private standing of one (or more) individual(s) against a State may trigger less political sensitivity. It also avoids the discretionary nature of a State claim, which may not be brought in case the violation of international economic obligations is considered not worth the risk of souring international relations in a different area.

Both ISDS and the WTO Dispute Settlement System seem to be grappling to find an answer to at least one area under scrutiny in this paper: how to reconcile broader public interest objectives with the specific purpose for which "their" dispute settlement mechanism was developed (investment and trade matters, respectively). No fully satisfactory solutions in this regard seem to have been found as of yet, but in their search for such solutions, ISDS tribunals and WTO Panels and the Appellate Body alike may wish to "look across the border" and closely follow the developments in each other's dispute settlement practice to find inspiration.

A Comment

Jacob GRIERSON[1]

When you invited me I knew nothing at all about WTO dispute settlement. I now know a lot more. It's a fascinating topic, so thank you very much.

Why didn't I know anything about WTO dispute settlement? Because I didn't take your class when I was here at the College – huge mistake – and so, instead of becoming a trade lawyer I became an international arbitration practitioner. I act as counsel and also as arbitrator in both commercial and investment disputes, and just to be clear about what is meant by an investment arbitration and a commercial arbitration: an investment arbitration is one which is either brought pursuant to a bilateral investment treaty or a multinational investment treaty such as the Energy Charter Treaty for example, or it can be one which is brought under a contract, typically an oil concession for example, in which the parties have agreed to submit their dispute to ICSID, which, as Professor Baetens explained, is a special body for deciding some of these disputes. Most of the bilateral investment treaties and the multinational ones as well give the option of going either to ICSID or to one or two or sometimes even three other institutions. ICSID is particular, as it is a totally self-contained system which doesn't require or indeed allow you to go to national courts. The New York Convention doesn't come into play, and that is exactly why Professor Baetens correctly distinguished between the two different types.

Now, being an international arbitration lawyer I am particularly interested in the two papers that have just been presented and I have a few comments on them. I will follow through the structure that has been followed in both papers.

First of all, concerning the appointment of arbitrators: I would submit that the problem of independence is in fact exaggerated. There are of course some arbitrators who are investor-friendly, but there are many others who are also very friendly to States. In fact, those who have been so virulently criticized for having always taken the side of one or the other, are in fact those who always sided with States, and there is one French law professor who particularly falls into that category.

---

[1]   Barrister, Partner of Mc Dermott Will & Emery (Paris).

On the whole it doesn't actually matter to have someone on the panel who's slightly biased. This may perhaps seem to be a surprising statement, but let's not forget that there are three arbitrators and at the end of the day the president has the casting vote and if, one of the co-arbitrators is known to be always on the side of States come what may, then obviously the president is going to discount that co-arbitrator's view to some extent. One issue that has arisen which is interesting in relation to independence is the question of issue estoppel. What various people have tried to do over the past ten or so years is to complain about the lack of independence of certain arbitrators based on views they've expressed in previous awards and in previous academic and other writings. None of those challenges has yet been successful. People say, well look, judges give judgments in which they express views, they write things and they don't get disqualified. Of course the difference is that you can't pick your judge before a national court, whereas you can pick your arbitrator. All this raises the very interesting question, whether it is right to have party-nominated arbitrators. And increasingly people are starting to ask this question. Jan Paulsson, a very well-known arbitrator, has recently written a paper which very strongly argues for getting rid of party-nominated arbitrators, and the reason basically is this: well, if the arbitrators are supposed to be impartial, not only independent but impartial, then what's the point of picking your arbitrator, unless of course, they're actually partial? Although it's not immediately easy to answer this argument, I personally feel very strongly that it's important to keep party-nominated arbitrators because, even if they're impartial, they will ensure that your client's case is properly heard. You can also choose an arbitrator whom you know or are familiar with and who will push for the kind of procedure that you want. For example, if you want more or less discovery, or a longer or shorter hearing, you'll pick the sort of person you know will have the same views that you have on that. So there are legitimate reasons for wanting to keep party-nominated arbitrators.

Secondly, concerning accountability – I'm going through the criticisms that Professor Baetens referred to: Arbitrators actually are pretty accountable. Their performance is very much scrutinized. It is scrutinized by their co-arbitrators if it's a panel of three who will always be looking carefully at their awards, unless they're asleep. It is scrutinized afterwards by counsel, who are the people that then go and compare notes on arbitrators at conferences. They are scrutinized sometimes by arbitral institutions. The ICC for example has a scrutiny process which is, I can tell you, pretty rigorous. And in the case of investment awards they are of course generally published. It's not always the case but it's getting better thanks to the 2013 UNCITRAL Rules. So there is in fact quite a lot of accountability of arbitrators.

Thirdly, concerning the lack of consistency of approach: for commercial arbitration obviously that doesn't matter because it's a private and confidential process and it doesn't concern anybody else. In terms of investment arbitration where, as I said, most of these awards, maybe not the pleadings, but the awards are in fact published, there is actually an enormous amount of consistency. When you do an investment arbitration it's totally different from doing a commercial arbitration for the simple reason that you spend a huge amount of time referring to other arbitral tribunals' case law. There's no system of *stare decisis* but nonetheless it is expected that the council will argue previous case law of other tribunals and that the tribunal will deal with that in their award, and they do. There are of course a few outliers in respect of each issue but the rest are pretty much in the same line and frankly it's not worse than what you get in between English High Court judges or with split circuits in the US. So I don't think there's a problem of lack of consistency.

Finally, concerning the appointment of arbitrators, let me comment on the idea of having a roster. Many people think it's a good idea to have a roster because at least that way you keep control of quality. I do not share that view because it merely entrenches the idea of a club and everybody who comes into contact with arbitration says "Oh but it's such a club, it's a closed shop, it's all the same people who know each other and have lunch with each other and want to do each other a favor". There is a bit of truth about this, and I believe that the club should open up, and having rosters is not going to help that at all.

I'm going to finish by saying that one thing that could be learnt in the world of WTO dispute settlement, which is definitely the case in arbitration, whether it's investment or commercial arbitration, is that you should have more academics sitting as arbitrators. I think that in the study we have been looking at it is showed that only thirty per cent of the WTO panel arbitrators are academics. In investment arbitration that's totally different: a very large number are in fact academics. And indeed in commercial arbitration many are academics as well and we find that they do a very good job as arbitrators.

College of Europe Studies

Europe is in a constant state of flux. European politics, economics, law and indeed European societies are changing rapidly. The European Union itself is in a continuous situation of adaptation. New challenges and new requirements arise continually, both internally and externally. The College of Europe Studies series exists to publish research on these issues done at the College of Europe, both at its Bruges and its Warsaw campus. Focused on the European Union and the European integration process, this research may be specialised in the areas of political science, law or economics, but much of it is of an interdisciplinary nature. The objective is to promote understanding of the issues concerned and to make a contribution to ongoing discussions.

Series Editors
Professors Olivier Costa, Inge Govaere, Sieglinde Gstöhl,
Phedon Nicolaides and Pascaline Winand

Series Titles

No. 12 – Jing MEN & Giuseppe BALDUCCI (eds.), *Prospects and Challenges for EU-China Relations in the 21ˢᵗ Century. The Partnership and Cooperation Agreement*, 2010, 262 p., ISBN 978-90-5201-641-2.

No. 11 – Jörg MONAR (ed.), *The Institutional Dimension of the European Union's Area of Freedom, Security and Justice*, 2010, p., ISBN 978-90-5201-615-3.

No. 10 – Dominik HANF, Klaus MALACEK & Elise MUIR (dir.), *Langues et construction européenne*, 2010, 286 p., ISBN 978-90-5201-594-1.

No. 9 – Jacques PELKMANS, Dominik HANF & Michele CHANG (eds.), *The EU Internal Market in Comparative Perspective. Economic, Political and Legal Analyses*, 2008, 314 p., ISBN 978-90-5201-424-1.

No. 8 – Inge GOVAERE & Hanns ULLRICH (eds.), *Intellectual Property, Market Power and the Public Interest*, 2008, 315 p., ISBN 978-90-5201-422-7.

No. 7 – András INOTAI, *The European Union and Southeastern Europe. Troubled Waters Ahead?*, 2007, 414 p., ISBN 978-90-5201-071-7.

No. 6 – Inge GOVAERE & Hanns ULLRICH (eds.), *Intellectual Property, Public Policy, and International Trade*, 2007, 234 p., ISBN 978-90-5201-064-9.

No. 5 – Dominik HANF & Rodolphe MUÑOZ (dir.), *La libre circulation des personnes. États des lieux et perspectives*, 2007, 329 p., ISBN 978-90-5201-061-8.

No. 4 – Dieter MAHNCKE & Sieglinde GSTÖHL (eds.), *Europe's Near Abroad. Promises and Prospects of the EU's Neighbourhood Policy*, 2008, 318 p., ISBN 978-90-5201-047-2.

No. 3 – Dieter MAHNCKE & Jörg MONAR (eds.), *International Terrorism. A European Response to a Global Threat?*, 2006, 191 p., ISBN 978-90-5201-046-5.

No. 2 – Paul DEMARET, Inge GOVAERE & Dominik HANF (eds.), *European Legal Dynamics – Revised and updated edition of* 30 Years of European Legal Studies at the College of Europe / *Dynamiques juridiques européennes – Édition revue et mise à jour de* 30 ans d'études juridiques européennes au Collège d'Europe, 2007, 571 p., ISBN 978-90-5201-067-0.

No. 1 – Dieter MAHNCKE, Alicia AMBOS & Christopher REYNOLDS (eds.), *European Foreign Policy. From Rhetoric to Reality?*, 2004, 2ⁿᵈ printing/ 2ᵉ tirage 2006, 381 p., ISBN 978-90-5201-247-6.

www.peterlang.com

Imprimé en France
FROC011743150620
24291FR00021B/274

9 782807 602878